高等职业院校汽车类规划教材编审委员会

编写指导专家　孙敬华
教材审定专家　李　雪
主　　　　任　姚道如
副　主　　任　汪　锐　余承辉　安宗权　何其宝　宋晓敏
委　　　　员（以姓氏笔画为序）

马　玲　王云霞　王治平　王爱国　凤鹏飞
刘荣富　江建刚　杜兰萍　杜淑琳　吴彩林
余永虎　汪永华　张信群　张善智　陈之林
陈传胜　金　明　段　伟　姜继文　娄　洁
柴宏钦　高　飞　高光辉　郭　微　黄道业
程　玉　程师苏　谢金忠　解　云　满维龙
慕　灿　戴　崇

高等职业院校汽车类规划教材

汽车专业英语

主　审　王爱国
主　编　王　利　黄昭明
副主编　李泽佳　张秀侠　耿　璐　陈中友
编写人员（以姓氏笔画为序）
　　　　王　利　王欢欢　李泽佳　张利芬
　　　　张秀侠　陈中友　耿　璐　黄昭明
　　　　韩二锋　谭　欣

中国科学技术大学出版社

内 容 简 介

本书以"系统改革、学以致用"为理念，建立了以高中英语为基础、从英语综合能力培养到职业实用英语学习、连续四个学期全过程渗透的递进式课程体系，确保学生不间断地学习英语。本课程能力标准以培养符合单位实际需要的高级应用型人才为原则，以培养具备解决实际问题能力的人才为出发点。本书以知识、能力、素养为主线设计教学内容，内容的设置满足了培养学生综合能力以及未来职业能力的需要，突出了高等职业教育的职业性、实用性和技能性等特色，更好地体现了高职公共英语专业教学服务的特征。

本书可作为高职高专院校汽车检测与维修、汽车电子技术、汽车技术服务与营销、汽车运用技术等专业的教材，也可作为普通高等学校汽车相关专业师生的学习和参考用书。

图书在版编目(CIP)数据

汽车专业英语/王利,黄昭明主编. —合肥:中国科学技术大学出版社,2017.1
ISBN 978-7-312-03981-2

Ⅰ. 汽… Ⅱ. ①王… ②黄… Ⅲ. 汽车工程—英语—高等职业教育—教材 Ⅳ. H31

中国版本图书馆 CIP 数据核字(2016)第 122749 号

出版　中国科学技术大学出版社
　　　安徽省合肥市金寨路96号,230026
　　　http://press.ustc.edu.cn
印刷　安徽省瑞隆印务有限公司
发行　中国科学技术大学出版社
经销　全国新华书店
开本　787 mm×1092 mm　1/16
印张　12
字数　399千
版次　2017年1月第1版
印次　2017年1月第1次印刷
定价　28.00元

Preface
序

安徽省示范性高等职业院校合作委员会（Cooperative Commission of Vocational Colleges Under Model Construction in Anhui Province），简称"A联盟"，由安徽省教育厅牵头组建，以国家示范、省示范高等职业院校为主体，坚持"交流、合作、开放、引领"的理念，连接政府、学校与社会，以实现优势互补、互惠互利、资源共享，构建安徽省示范院校交流与合作的平台，引领和深化安徽省高等职业教育的改革与发展。

"A联盟"汽车类专业建设协作组（皖高示范合〔2012〕5号）是安徽省示范性高等职业院校合作委员会中的一个专业指导组，在"A联盟"指导下负责安徽省高职汽车类专业教学的研究和指导。组长由安徽职业技术学院姚道如教授担任，副组长分别由安徽水利水电职业技术学院余承辉教授、芜湖职业技术学院安宗权副教授、六安职业技术学院何其宝副教授担任，秘书长由安徽汽车职业技术学院宋晓敏主任担任。关于汽车专业课程建设，"A联盟"多次召开会议讨论，并根据《高等职业学校专业教学标准（试行）》制定了汽车类专业课程体系，成立了教材编审委员会，编写系列教材。此套教材具有下列特色：

1. 为安徽省示范性高等职业院校合作委员会规划教材。

教材的研究、开发、推广及应用是以"A联盟"为平台的，主编和参编人员均为"A联盟"一线骨干教师。

2. 以标准为准绳。

教材以教育部职业教育与成人教育司最新发布的《高等职业学校专业教学标准（试行）》为准绳，以汽车行业标准为依据，并结合安徽省实际情况展开编写。

3. 体现校企合作。

参与教材编写的企业人员为奇瑞汽车股份有限公司、江淮汽车股份有限公司及安徽汽车贸易公司等企业的技术骨干。

4. 紧跟产业升级。

将新工艺、新结构、新技术、新管理等引入教材，贴近汽车企业生产、工艺、维修、销售等实际情况。

5. 编写理念新，具有"教、学、做"的可操作性。

教材根据相应课程特点，采用适合的编写模式编写：专业及核心课程采用项目或任务驱动等模式编写，而公共基础课程采用章节形式编写。在编写过程中充分考虑实际教学中

"教、学、做"的可操作性。

6. 体现中、高职衔接。

教材内容选取、专业能力培养、方法能力培养、社会能力培养以及评价标准体现中、高职衔接的发展方向。

该套教材的出版将服务高职院校汽车类专业教育教学改革，促进汽车类专业高端技能人才的培养。

安徽省示范性高等职业院校合作委员会汽车专业协作组

2013 年 6 月 11 日

Foreword
前　　言

  汽车专业英语是汽车检测与维修、汽车电子技术、汽车技术服务与营销等专业的公共基础课程，支撑相关专业职业能力的发展，在汽车专业中起着举足轻重的作用。通过较系统地学习汽车专业英语知识，学生能够熟练掌握汽车后服务行业维修、营销等职业岗位工作所必需的英语词汇，具备阅读和翻译汽车行业英语使用说明书和有关技术手册的能力；同时，能够运用互联网查询相关专业英语资料，达到汽车后服务行业职业岗位对英语的要求；最终能够通过使用英语更好地从事汽车相关的职业。

  本书中每个单元均包括以下几个部分内容，特色鲜明。

  第一部分为图解英语（Illustrated English），包括若干幅图片，注重趣味性、直观性和实用性，以提高学生的学习兴趣，使学生能够满足未来从业时市场对从业者的客观要求。

  第二部分为专业阅读（Technical and Practical Reading），包括一篇精选文章，可以帮助学生了解汽车各部分的功能及应用，是学生进入企业后应用较多的必学内容。

  第三部分为交际会话（Listening and Speaking），包括两篇精选对话，选用贴近实际、贴近企业、贴近岗位的常用专业英语会话，用于提高学生的口语交际能力。

  第四部分为阅读材料（Reading Material），将专业阅读的知识进行适当拓展，内容涉及一些相关的、有趣的、发展方向性的新技术、新方法、新原理等。

  本书由王利与黄昭明主编，王爱国主审。全书共分为17个单元。其中，第1至第3单元及单词索引由河海大学文天学院黄昭明编写，第4、第5单元由合肥职业技术学院耿璐编写，第6、第7单元由泸州职业技术学院李泽佳编写，第8、第9单元由安庆职业技术学院张秀侠编写，第10单元由阜阳职业技术学院王欢欢编写；第11、第12单元由宣城职业技术学院王利编写，第13、第14单元由重庆安全技术职业学院谭欣编写，第15单元由芜湖职业技术学院张利芬编写，第16单元由浙江农业商贸职业学院韩二锋编写，第17单元由枣庄职业技术学院陈中友编写。

  由于编者经历及水平所限，书中不当与疏漏之处在所难免，恳请读者提出宝贵意见，以便再版时及时更正。

编　者
2016年3月

Contents
目　录

Preface ··· (i)

Foreword ·· (iii)

Unit 1　Automobile Construction ·· (1)
Part Ⅰ　Illustrated English ·· (1)
　Diagram of Automobile Construction ·· (1)
Part Ⅱ　Technical and Practical Reading ··· (2)
　Structure of Automobile ·· (2)
Part Ⅲ　Listening and Speaking ··· (7)
　Project Planning A ·· (7)
　Project Planning B ·· (8)
Part Ⅳ　Reading Material ·· (9)
　History of the Automobile ·· (9)

Unit 2　Automobile Engines ··· (11)
Part Ⅰ　Illustrated English ·· (11)
　Diagram of Gasoline Engine's Basic Structure ·· (11)
Part Ⅱ　Technical and Practical Reading ··· (12)
　Automobile Engines ·· (12)
Part Ⅲ　Listening and Speaking ··· (17)
　SWOT Analysis A ·· (17)
　SWOT Analysis B ·· (17)
Part Ⅳ　Reading Material ·· (18)
　Different Types of Engines ··· (18)

Unit 3　Crank Connecting Rod Mechanism and Body Group ···························· (21)
Part Ⅰ　Illustrated English ·· (21)
　Diagram of Crank Connecting Rod Mechanism and Body Group ················ (21)
Part Ⅱ　Technical and Practical Reading ··· (22)
　Valve Train ··· (22)
Part Ⅲ　Listening and Speaking ··· (26)
　Market Research A ··· (26)

Market Research B ……………………………………………………… (27)
　Part Ⅳ　Reading Material ………………………………………………… (28)
　　Crankshaft and Connecting Rod Mechanism ……………………………… (28)

Unit 4　Ventilation System and Gas Exchange Process ……………… (30)
　Part Ⅰ　Illustrated English …………………………………………… (30)
　　Diagram of Ventilation System's Structure ……………………………… (30)
　Part Ⅱ　Technical and Practical Reading ……………………………… (31)
　　Structure of Ventilation System ………………………………………… (31)
　Part Ⅲ　Listening and Speaking ………………………………………… (37)
　　Automotive Design A …………………………………………………… (37)
　　Automotive Design B …………………………………………………… (38)
　Part Ⅳ　Reading Material ………………………………………………… (39)
　　Air Exchange Process and Variable Valve Timing ……………………… (39)

Unit 5　Supply and Combustion of Gasoline Engine Fuel …………… (41)
　Part Ⅰ　Illustrated English …………………………………………… (41)
　　Diagram of Gasoline Engine Fuel System ………………………………… (41)
　Part Ⅱ　Technical and Practical Reading ……………………………… (42)
　　Engine Gasoline Supply System ………………………………………… (42)
　Part Ⅲ　Listening and Speaking ………………………………………… (47)
　　Automotive Testing A …………………………………………………… (47)
　　Automotive Testing B …………………………………………………… (47)
　Part Ⅳ　Reading Material ………………………………………………… (48)
　　Lean Combustion Technology and Cylinder Direct Injection Electronic Control
　　Technology ……………………………………………………………… (48)

Unit 6　Supply and Combustion of Diesel Engine Fuel ………………… (51)
　Part Ⅰ　Illustrated English …………………………………………… (51)
　　Diagram of Diesel Engine Fuel System …………………………………… (51)
　Part Ⅱ　Technical and Practical Reading ……………………………… (52)
　　Electronically Controlled Diesel Injection System ……………………… (52)
　Part Ⅲ　Listening and Speaking ………………………………………… (57)
　　Manufacturing Process A ………………………………………………… (57)
　　Manufacturing Process B ………………………………………………… (58)
　Part Ⅳ　Reading Material ………………………………………………… (58)
　　Combustion of Diesel Engine …………………………………………… (58)

Unit 7　Gasoline Engine Ignition System ……………………………… (61)
　Part Ⅰ　Illustrated English …………………………………………… (61)

	Diagram of Engine Ignition System with and without Distributor	(61)
Part II	Technical and Practical Reading	(62)
	Ignition System and Starting System	(62)
Part III	Listening and Speaking	(68)
	Automotive Outsourcing A	(68)
	Automotive Outsourcing B	(69)
Part IV	Reading Material	(70)
	Automotive Electrical System	(70)

Unit 8 Engine Emission Control System (73)

Part I	Illustrated English	(73)
	Diagram of Engine Emission System	(73)
Part II	Technical and Practical Reading	(74)
	Engine Emission Control System	(74)
Part III	Listening and Speaking	(79)
	Automotive Outsourcing A	(79)
	Automotive Outsourcing B	(80)
Part IV	Reading Material	(81)
	Vehicle emission control in China	(81)

Unit 9 Engine Cooling System (83)

Part I	Illustrated English	(83)
	Diagram of Engine Cooling System	(83)
Part II	Technical and Practical Reading	(83)
	Engine Cooling System	(83)
Part III	Listening and Speaking	(89)
	Production Supervision A	(89)
	Production Supervision B	(90)
Part IV	Reading Material	(91)
	Air Conditioner	(91)

Unit 10 Engine Lubricating System (93)

Part I	Illustrated English	(93)
	Diagram of Engine Lubricating System	(93)
Part II	Technical and Practical Reading	(93)
	Engine Lubricating System	(93)
Part III	Listening and Speaking	(98)
	Production Safety A	(98)
	Production Safety B	(99)
Part IV	Reading Material	(100)

  Classification of Lubrication Oils ……………………………………………… (100)

Unit 11 New Type Automobile Engine ……………………………………… (103)
 Part Ⅰ Illustrated English ……………………………………………………… (103)
  Diagram of New Power Vehicle ……………………………………………… (103)
 Part Ⅱ Technical and Practical Reading ……………………………………… (104)
  Electric Vehicle ………………………………………………………………… (104)
 Part Ⅲ Listening and Speaking ………………………………………………… (108)
  New Technologies A …………………………………………………………… (108)
  New Technologies B …………………………………………………………… (110)
 Part Ⅳ Reading Material ………………………………………………………… (110)
  Hybrid Electric Vehicle ………………………………………………………… (110)

Unit 12 Manual Transmissions ……………………………………………… (114)
 Part Ⅰ Illustrated English ……………………………………………………… (114)
  Diagram of Manual Transmissions Structure ……………………………… (114)
 Part Ⅱ Technical and Practical Reading ……………………………………… (115)
  Manual Transmissions ………………………………………………………… (115)
 Part Ⅲ Listening and Speaking ………………………………………………… (118)
  Introduction of New Models A ……………………………………………… (118)
  Introduction of New Models B ……………………………………………… (119)
 Part Ⅳ Reading Material ………………………………………………………… (120)
  Dual Clutch Transmission …………………………………………………… (120)

Unit 13 Automatic Transmissions ………………………………………… (123)
 Part Ⅰ Illustrated English ……………………………………………………… (123)
  Diagram of Automatic Transmissions ……………………………………… (123)
 Part Ⅱ Technical and Practical Reading ……………………………………… (124)
  Automatic Transmissions …………………………………………………… (124)
 Part Ⅲ Listening and Speaking ………………………………………………… (131)
  Negotiation of Price A ………………………………………………………… (131)
  Negotiation of Price B ………………………………………………………… (132)
 Part Ⅳ Reading Material ………………………………………………………… (132)
  Continuously Variable Transmission ………………………………………… (132)

Unit 14 Steering System …………………………………………………… (135)
 Part Ⅰ Illustrated English ……………………………………………………… (135)
  Diagram of Steering System ………………………………………………… (135)
 Part Ⅱ Technical and Practical Reading ……………………………………… (136)
  Steering System ………………………………………………………………… (136)

Contents

　Part Ⅲ　Listening and Speaking ·· (139)
　　Maintenance A ·· (139)
　　Maintenance B ·· (140)
　Part Ⅳ　Reading Material ·· (140)
　　Types of Steering Gears ·· (140)

Unit 15　Suspension System ··· (143)
　Part Ⅰ　Illustrated English ·· (143)
　　Diagram of Suspension System ··· (143)
　Part Ⅱ　Technical and Practical Reading ······································· (144)
　　Suspension System ··· (144)
　Part Ⅲ　Listening and Speaking ·· (148)
　　Steering system A ·· (148)
　　Steering system B ·· (149)
　Part Ⅳ　Reading Material ·· (149)
　　Industry Overview ·· (149)

Unit 16　Braking System ··· (151)
　Part Ⅰ　Illustrated English ·· (151)
　　Diagram of Braking System and ABS ·· (151)
　Part Ⅱ　Technical and Practical Reading ······································· (152)
　　Braking System ··· (152)
　Part Ⅲ　Listening and Speaking ·· (158)
　　Crash Sensor A ·· (158)
　　Crash Sensor B ·· (158)
　Part Ⅳ　Reading Material ·· (159)
　　How F1 Brakes Work ·· (159)

Unit 17　Sensors ··· (162)
　Part Ⅰ　Illustrated English ·· (162)
　　Diagram of Sensors of Automobile Engine and Power System ······ (162)
　Part Ⅱ　Technical and Practical Reading ······································· (163)
　　Sensors ··· (163)
　Part Ⅲ　Listening and Speaking ·· (168)
　　Information About a New Car A ·· (168)
　　Information About a New Car B ·· (169)
　Part Ⅳ　Reading Material ·· (170)
　　OBD Ⅱ and DLC ·· (170)

Index ··· (172)

Unit 1　Automobile Construction

Part Ⅰ　Illustrated English

Diagram of Automobile Construction

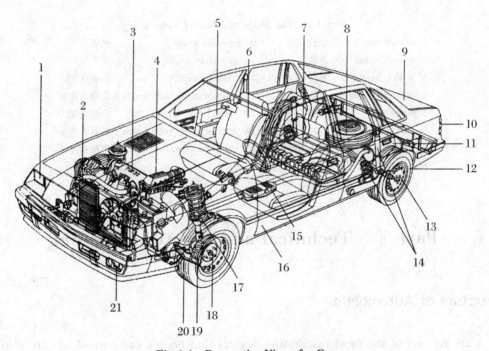

Fig. 1-1　Perspective View of a Car

1. head lamp　前照灯
2. radiator　散热器
3. engine　发动机
4. air cleaner　空气滤清器
5. door　车门
6. seat　座椅
7. fuel tank　燃油箱
8. spare tire　备胎
9. body　车身
10. tail light　尾灯
11. muffler　消声器
12. tire　轮胎
13. wheel rim　轮辋
14. rear suspension　后悬架
15. catalytic converter　催化转化器
16. front sill panel　前门槛
17. front suspension　前悬架
18. front wheel hub　前轮毂
19. front brake　前制动器
20. control arm　控制臂
21. turn signal lamp　转向信号灯

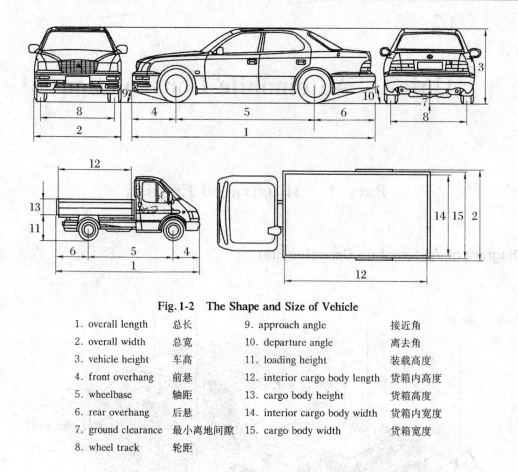

Fig. 1-2 The Shape and Size of Vehicle

1. overall length 总长
2. overall width 总宽
3. vehicle height 车高
4. front overhang 前悬
5. wheelbase 轴距
6. rear overhang 后悬
7. ground clearance 最小离地间隙
8. wheel track 轮距
9. approach angle 接近角
10. departure angle 离去角
11. loading height 装载高度
12. interior cargo body length 货箱内高度
13. cargo body height 货箱高度
14. interior cargo body width 货箱内宽度
15. cargo body width 货箱宽度

Part II   Technical and Practical Reading

Structure of Automobile

  Cars are one of the most fascinating devices that people can own. Cars are also one of the most pervasive devices, with a typical American family owning two cars.

  A car contains dozens of different technologies. Everything from the engine to the tires is its own special universe of design and engineering. But any automobiles are made up of four basic sections: engine, chassis, body and electrical system.

  The automobile engine is an internal combustion engine which converts the heat energy of fuel into mechanical energy to make the car move. In the internal combustion engine, the combustible mixture is compressed and then burned inside the engine cylinders. The burning of air-fuel mixture produces high pressure which forces piston to move downward. The movement is transmitted to the crankshaft by the connecting rod. The crankshaft is made to rotate then. The rotary motion is carried through the power train to the wheels so that they run and the car moves.

As the source of power, the engine requires a fuel system to supply with fuel or the mixture of air and fuel. It plays a vital role in the power-producing process. Suppose the engine is a gasoline engine, the fuel system pumps liquid gasoline from a tank into the carburetor where the gasoline can be mixed with air. The mixture is delivered to the engine where it is burned. If the engine is EFI (electronic fuel injection) engine, fuel is delivered from the tank to the injector by means of an electric fuel pump. The fuel injectors, which directly control fuel metering to the intake manifold, is pulsed by the ECU (electronic Control Unit). The ECU determines air-fuel ratio of the engine according to engine condition.

The engine also needs a cooling system, because the combustion of the air-fuel mixture in the engine creates a very high temperature (as high as 2 000 ℃ to 2 700 ℃). The cooling system takes heat away from the engine by either circulating liquid coolant (water mixed with antifreeze) between the engine and the radiator, or passing air through the radiator. Today, liquid-cooled engines are common. It cools off as it goes through the radiator. Thus, the coolant continually takes heat away from the engine, where it could do damage, and delivers it to the radiator.

The engine also includes a lubricating system. The purpose of the lubricating system is to supply all moving parts inside the engine with lubricating oil; the oil keeps moving parts from wearing excessively.

The engine has a starting system. Its purpose is to change the electrical current into the mechanical energy to push the crankshaft around. By means of this, the engine can be started.

The way to produce heat energy is different between gasoline and diesel engines. There is only an ignition system in gasoline engine. The ignition system provides high-voltage electric sparks that set fire to the charges of air-fuel mixture in the engine combustion chambers. However, the heat energy for igniting the charges is created within the diesel engine by compressing pure air to a degree that will initiate combustion and then injecting the fuel at the right time in relation to the movement of the crankshaft.

A chassis which is considered as a support frame for an auto body is used to assemble all auto spare parts on it. In fact, when power from engine continues to be transmitted to chassis, it begins with power train, goes on to steering, wheel suspension, brakes and tires. These individual components interact with each other closely. Therefore, a chassis itself can be divided into the following systems.

Driving system connects the transmission with the driving axle. In effect, the driving system works by transmitting engine power to the driving wheels. The driving system consists of clutch, transmission, universal joint, driving axle, etc.

Steering system is used to control the driving direction of an automobile. It is composed of steering wheel, steering column, worm gear sector, steering knuckle arm and worm.

Brake system is a balanced set of mechanical and hydraulic devices used to retard the motion of the vehicle by means of friction. It consists of drum or disc brake assembly, brake lever assembly, etc.

An Anti-lock Brake System (ABS) is a computer-controlled brake system that helps prevent wheel lockup during braking. ABS can maintain control of the vehicle. It works by limiting the pressure to any wheel, which decelerates too rapidly. This allows maximum stopping force to be applied without brake lockup. "ASR" stands for "Acceleration Slip Regulation", and it is the way of guaranteeing that the wheels have equal traction when you need to accelerate quickly.

The automobile body which is regarded as the framework is seated on the chassis. Its function is obvious, to provide comfort, protection and shelter for occupants. The automobile body is generally divided into four sections: the front, the upper or the top, the rear and the underbody. These sections are further divided into small units, such as the hood, the fenders, the roof panels, the door, the instrument panel, the bumpers and the luggage compartment.

The electrical system is considered as an auto electric power source supplies lighting power for the automobile. The electrical system contains battery, lights, generator, engine ignition, lighting circuit, and various switches that control their use.

With the rapid development of automobile industry, the new models of automobiles are becoming better and better in design and performance. When automobiles are very popular with people, many negative problems corresponding to the facts have to be considered by scientists, such as energy crisis, air pollution and traffic jam. So scientists and auto manufacturers are doing their best to improve fuel economy, control exhaust emissions; the governments are taking active measures to solve traffic problems at the same time.

New Words

1. fascinating ['fæsɪˌneɪtɪŋ] adj. 迷人的,吸引人的
2. pervasive [pər'veɪsɪv] adj. 遍及的,弥漫的
3. engine ['ɛndʒɪn] n. 发动机
4. chassis ['ʃæsi] n. 底盘
5. body ['bɑːdi] n. 车身
6. combustion [kəm'bʌstʃən] n. 燃烧
7. combustible [kəm'bʌstəbəl] adj. 易燃的,易激动的
8. cylinder ['sɪlɪndə(r)] n. 气缸
9. piston ['pɪstən] n. 活塞
10. crankshaft ['kræŋkʃæft] n. 曲轴
11. rotate ['roʊteɪt] v. 旋转
12. vital ['vaɪtl] adj. 至关重要的
13. tank [tæŋk] n. 油箱
14. suppose [sə'poʊz] v. 假定,推测
15. pulse [pʌls] vt. 用脉冲输送
16. coolant ['kuːlənt] n. 冷冻剂,冷却液
17. radiator ['reɪdiˌeɪtə] n. 散热器,水箱
18. lubricate ['luːbrɪˌkeɪt] v. 润滑
19. wear [wer] v. 磨损

20. gasoline ['gæsəlin] n. 汽油
21. diesel ['dizəl] n. 柴油机
22. ignition [ɪg'nɪʃən] n. 点火,点着
23. voltage ['voʊltɪdʒ] n. 电压
24. spark [spɑːrk] n. 火花
25. charge [tʃɑːrdʒ] n. 填充物
26. suspension [sə'spɛnʃən] n. 悬架
27. brake [brek] n. 制动器,刹车
28. tire [taɪr] n. 轮胎
29. interact [ˌɪntɚ'ækt] v. 相互作用,相互影响
30. transmission [træns'mɪʃən] n. 变速器
31. clutch [klʌtʃ] n. 离合器
32. hydraulic [haɪ'drɔlɪk] adj. 液压的
33. drum [drʌm] n. 鼓
34. disc [dɪsk] n. 盘
35. lockup ['lɑkˌʌp] n. 锁定,锁住
36. decelerate [di'sɛləˌret] v.（使）减速
37. guarantee [ˌgærən'ti] v. 保证,抵押,担保
38. hood [hʊd] n. 发动机罩
39. fender ['fɛndɚ] n. 挡泥板
40. underbody [ˈʌndəˌbʌdɪ] n. 底板
41. bumper ['bʌmpɚ] n. 保险杠
42. luggage ['lʌgɪdʒ] n. 行李
43. battery ['bætəri] n. 蓄电池
44. generator ['dʒɛnəˌretɚ] n. 发电机

Phrases and Expressions

1. electrical system　电气系统
2. internal combustion engine　内燃机
3. combustible mixture　可燃混合物
4. connecting rod　连杆
5. EFI engine　电喷发动机
6. fuel injector　喷油器
7. intake manifold　进气歧管
8. ECU　电子控制单元
9. air-fuel ratio　空燃比
10. cooling system　冷却系统
11. lubricating system　润滑系统
12. lubricating oil　润滑油
13. starting system　起动系统
14. ignition system　点火系统
15. auto spare part　汽车零部件
16. power train　传动系统
17. driving system　行驶系统
18. universal joint　万向节
19. driving axle　驱动桥,传动轴
20. steering system　转向系统
21. steering wheel　方向盘
22. steering column　转向柱
23. worm gear sector　扇形轮
24. steering drop arm　转向垂臂
25. brake lever assembly　制动杆总成
26. Anti-lock Brake System（ABS）　制动防抱死系统
27. Acceleration Slip Regulation（ASR）驱动防滑转系统
28. roof panel　（车身）顶板
29. lighting circuit　照明系统
30. traffic jam　交通堵塞
31. fuel economy　燃油经济性

Notes to Text

1. A car contains dozens of different technologies. Everything from the engine to the tires is its own special universe of design and engineering.

一辆车包含了多种不同的技术。从发动机到轮胎,每一个零部件都有其专门的设计和工程技术领域。

2. Suppose the engine is a gasoline engine, the fuel system pumps liquid gasoline from a tank into the carburetor where the gasoline can be mixed with air.

假设发动机为汽油机,燃油供给系统会把油箱里的液态汽油输送到化油器,这个化油器能将汽油与空气混合。

3. The purpose of the lubrication system is to supply all moving parts inside the engine with lubricating oil; the oil keeps moving parts from wearing excessively.

润滑系统的作用是给发动机内部的运动部件提供润滑油;润滑油可避免运动部件过度磨损。

4. The ignition system provides high-voltage electric sparks that set fire to ignite the air-fuel mixture in the engine combustion chambers.

点火系统产生高压电火花,能够点燃发动机燃烧室内的可燃混合物。

5. However, the heat energy for igniting the charge is created within the diesel engine by compressing pure air to a degree that will initiate combustion and then injecting the fuel at right time in relation to the movement of the crankshaft.

可是,在柴油机发动机中,燃油点火的热量是靠将空气压缩到可以引燃的程度来产生的,并在对应于曲轴转动的恰当时刻喷入燃料。

6. A chassis which is considered as a support frame for an auto body is used to assembly all auto spare parts on it.

底盘被用来总装汽车零部件,它被认为是车身的支架。

7. "ASR" stands for "Acceleration Slip Regulation", and it is the way of guaranteeing that the wheels have equal traction when you need to accelerate quickly.

"ASR"的意思是"驱动防滑系统",它是当你急需加速时保证每个车轮有相等的地面附着力的措施。

Exercises

1. Answer the following questions to the text.

(1) What is the function of the automobile engine?

(2) What is the steering system composed of?

(3) What do ABS and ASR mean?

(4) Is the way to produce the heat energy different between gasoline and diesel engines? Why?

(5) What disadvantages does the automobile bring us?

2. Translate the following phrases and expressions into Chinese.

(1) exhaust emission

(2) fuel economy

(3) roof panel

(4) combustible mixture
(5) universal joint
(6) ABS
(7) ASR

3. Translate the following sentences into Chinese.

(1) A car contains dozens of different technologies. Everything from the engine to the tires is its own special universe of design and engineering.

(2) The automobile engine is an internal combustion engine which converts the heat energy of fuel into mechanical energy to make the car move.

(3) The cooling system takes heat away from the engine by either circulating a liquid coolant (water mixed with antifreeze) between the engine and the radiator, or passing air through the radiator.

(4) The engine has a starting system. Its purpose is to change the electrical current into the mechanical energy to push the crank-shaft around.

(5) In fact, when power from engine continues to be transmitted to chassis, it begins with power train, goes on to steering, wheel suspension, brakes and tires. These individual components interact with each other closely.

(6) An Anti-lock Brake System (ABS) is a computer-controlled brake system that helps prevent wheel lockup during braking.

Part Ⅲ Listening and Speaking

Project Planning A

A—Investor B—Manager

A: We feel the market will soon be on the upgrade. So, it's time to work together on a new model.
B: I think we all agree that there will be a market boom soon, and what's more, some types of our cars are gradually in decline. Though we can save them by re-invention, the best way is to find a replacement. If we plan ahead, we shall beat out competitors.
A: Yes. When people start spending the money, they save the market slump. We'll do well.
B: We're ready to put a lot of money into making the product. Are you going to invest in marketing to develop the market for it?
A: Yes. Our company is not making much money now, but we know if we spend money to develop the market for this product, the future profits will be good.

B: It's a feature of the market that people start to buy things only when they are sure the market is getting better.
A: I think we have an agreement on this point. All we need is a new type of car which will be our hit product.
B: Yes. We are working on it. We're going to design a new type of SUV according to the market need survey. We will show you our new project planning on this new type of car next time.

Project Planning B

A—John   B—Marsha   C—Manager

A: It's seven o'clock, and I want to call the annual share holders meeting to order. Every one was mailed an agenda and notice of the meeting over ten days ago. Those documents were also available when you checked in tonight. The first item of business on the agenda tonight is the developing of the new type of mid-end family car. I think Marsha is ready with a brief verbal report. Is that right, Marsha?
B: Yes, I'm all set.
A: Good, Marsh has the floor.
B: Thank you, John. I assume everyone has got a copy of project planning. I'm here today to present our new model developing planning. I will have a brief introduction about this planning. In order to enrich the market share of our car in this city, we are supposed to develop a car which caters for the majority of consumers. To roll out a new model of family car is the theme of this project planning. In this plan, I give a simple instruction on the project scope and developing cycle time, distributing the developing resources and so on. Well, thank you for your attention, do you have any questions?
C: So, what's our target audience?
B: We will focus on the mid-class families.
C: But our former models are inclined to the upper-level income consumers.
B: That's right. Whereas, according to the demographic report, our crowd in other cities is a quite different make-up from this city. You can see it from the pie chart on the fifth page. Obviously, the consumers in other more developed cities are mostly from middle to high income levels, university or postgraduates, white collar … you know the kind. This city on the other hand is mostly to low income levels, blue collar … I think we're talking about two totally different target groups. So, the car model introduced should fit for the specific consumers.
C: I had no idea there was that great of a deviation … To make our new car sell, we have to take the target audience into account.
B: No kidding. The first thing we do is to develop a most suitable car to fulfill the needs of the major consumers. In this project planning, I provide a copy of SWOT analysis

about developing a mid-end model.

C: Thanks for the presentation. I think what we need now is a more detailed project plan.

B: No problem. A copy of detailed project planning will be on your desk next Monday.

Part IV   Reading Material

History of the Automobile

The automobile industry is one of the most important industries affecting not only the economy but also the culture of the world. The manufacture, the sale and the servicing of automobiles have become the key elements of industrial economy. Automobiles revolutionized transportation in the 20th century, changing thoroughly the way people live, travel and do business.

Automobiles are classified by size, style, number of doors and intended use. The typical automobile, also called car, auto, motor car and passenger car, has four wheels and can carry up to five people including a driver. Vehicles designed to carry more passengers are called cargo, also called vans, minivans, omnibuses or buses. Those used to carry cargo are called pickups or trucks, depending on their size and design. Sport-utility vehicles, also known as SUV, are designed for driving in mud or snow.

Today automobile production has grown from small workshops making simple horseless carriages to international corporations that mass-produce advanced automobiles. Automobiles are the products of centuries of innovations and improvements.

Steam-powered Vehicles

In the 15th century, Italian inventor Leonardo da Vinci envisioned the possibilities for power-driver vehicles. By the late 17th century, English physicist Sir Isaac Newton had proposed a steam carriage, and in 1769 French army captain Nicholas-Joseph Cugnot actually built one — a steam-powered, three-wheeled tractor that was used to haul military equipment at the speed of 2.5 miles per hour. Later, he designed another vehicle to carry people. Other inventors made many improvements to vehicles in the following several decades. Steam-powered stagecoaches were in regular service in many towns in Britain in the early 1800s. Half a century later, the popularity of steam vehicles began to decline because they were dangerous to operate and difficult to maintain.

Electricity-powered Vehicles

From 1832 to 1839, Scottish inventor Robert Anderson designed a more practical vehicle that used a battery to power a small motor. This was hailed as a breakthrough, even though this vehicle was still very slow and often needed to stop for a recharge. But the idea of electricity-powered vehicles did catch on. Streetcars and trams used electricity for power and became the most popular transportation mode of choice in Europe and the U.S. in the mid-1800s.

Gasoline-powered Vehicles

It was the invention of the gasoline-powered engine that really brought a reliable and workable automobile to the world. Gasoline-powered engines were not new; some of the first designs could be dated back to the late 1700s. Some inventors attempted to make a wagon or a carriage run by a motor, but with moderate success.

In 1885, Karl Benz built the first three-wheeled gasoline-powered car in Germany. In the following year, the milestone vehicle was built by Gottlieb Daimler, another German. He perfected the two-cylinder gasoline engine and attached it to a stagecoach, thereby producing the first four-wheeled motor vehicle in the world. And then, engineers and designers went on with refining and shaping the engine and vehicle designs. By the early 1900s, motor-powered vehicles had become more popular than any other type of vehicles.

The First Vehicle Workshop

In 1889, former woodworkers Rene Panhard and Emile Levassor in France set up the first workshop that built complete motor vehicles. They made each new car a little bit different from its predecessors for years. Cars were refined during processing. Improvements included moving the engine to the front of the vehicle and designing a rear-wheel drive for better control of the vehicle.

Mass-produced Vehicles

In 1913, Henry Ford began making automobiles on a moving conveyor line in his factories. He realized that efficient mass production could lower car prices, making cars affordable for the average people, thus generating a huge market. This was a smashing success. By 1916 annual U.S. auto production reached one million units, a level not reached by any other country until about 40 years later in England.

Still Growing

Today, auto-making has become the world's largest manufacturing activity, with nearly 58 million new vehicles built each year worldwide. Besides, many other industries support the automobile industry. By some estimates, for every job created in the automobile assembly line, three to four jobs are created in the automotive parts industry. The automobile industry is surely an important source of employment and transportation for billions of people. The 1900s can be called the Age of Automobile, and cars will no doubt continue to shape our culture and economy well into the whole 21st century.

Unit 2 Automobile Engines

Part Ⅰ Illustrated English

Diagram of Gasoline Engine's Basic Structure

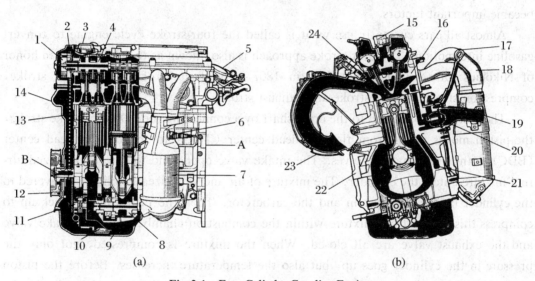

Fig. 2-1 Four-Cylinder Gasoline Engine

1. variable valve timing 可变气门正时
2. cylinder head cover 气缸盖罩
3. oil filler cap 机油加注口盖
4. camshaft 凸轮轴
5. throttle body 节气门体
6. O_2S (= oxygen sensor) 氧传感器
7. catalytic converter 催化转化器
8. balance shaft 平衡轴
9. oil pan 油底壳
10. oil strainer 机油集滤器
11. oil pump 机油泵
12. camshaft timing sprocket 凸轮轴正时链轮
13. timing chain 正时链条
14. timing chain cover 正时链条罩
15. ignition coil 点火线圈
16. cylinder head 缸盖,气缸盖
17. oil dipstick 机油尺
18. exhaust gas manifold 排气歧管
19. outlet spout 出水管
20. thermostat 节温器
21. jacket 水套
22. cylinder block 缸体,气缸体
23. intake air manifold 进气歧管
24. injector 喷油器
A. rear of engine 发动机后面
B. front of engine 发动机前面

Part II Technical and Practical Reading

Automobile Engines

The reciprocating piston internal combustion system has been the most successful for automobiles, while diesel engines are widely used for trucks and buses. The gasoline engine was originally selected for the automobile due to its flexibility over a wide range of speeds. Also, the power developed for a given weight engine was reasonable; it could be produced by economical mass production methods; and it used a readily available, moderately priced fuel-gasoline. Reliability, compact size and range of operation later became important factors.

Almost all cars currently use what is called the four-stroke cycle engine to convert gasoline into motion. The four-stroke approach is also known as the Otto cycle, in honor of Nikolaus Otto, who invented it in 1867. The four strokes are intake stroke, compression stroke, power stroke and exhaust stroke.

The piston is connected to the crankshaft by a connecting rod. On the intake stroke, the piston moves down from the top dead center (TDC) to the bottom dead center (BDC) as the crankshaft revolves. The intake valve opens and the fresh vaporized air-fuel mixture enters the cylinder. The mixture of air and vaporized gasoline is delivered to the cylinder by the fuel system and the carburetor. Then the piston moves back up to compress this combustible mixture within the combustion chamber and the intake valve and the exhaust valve are all closed. When the mixture is compressed, not only the pressure in the cylinder goes up, but also the temperature increases. Before the piston reaches TDC on the compression stroke, the spark plug emits a spark to ignite the mixture. The gasoline charge in the cylinder explodes, driving the piston down. At the same time, the crankshaft is rotated as the piston is pushed down by the pressure above it. Finally, once the piston hits near the BDC, the exhaust valve opens. Then the piston again moves up in the cylinder and the burned gas are pushed out. The intake valve usually opens before the end of exhaust stroke. When the piston again moves downward to BDC, the fresh combustible mixture will be introduced into the cylinder. The above four strokes are continuously repeated as long as the engine remains running. Notice that the linear motion of the pistons in an engine is converted into rotational motion by the crankshaft. The rotational motion is nice because we plan to rotate the car's wheels with it anyway.

The core of the engine is the cylinder, with the piston moving up and down inside the cylinder. The engine described above has one cylinder. That is typical of most lawn mowers, but most cars have more than one cylinder (four, six and eight cylinders are common). In a multi-cylinder engine, the cylinders usually are arranged in one of the three ways: in-line, V-type and flat (also known as horizontally opposed). As the in-line engine, cylinders may be arranged in a straight line one behind the other. The most automotive in-line designs have the four- and six-cylinder engines. The V-type engine has two banks of cylinders which have an inclination of 60 to 90 degrees. The cylinders of each bank are arranged one behind the other. The most common examples have six or eight cylinders. The flat engine has two banks of cylinders opposed each other horizontally. Different configurations have different advantages and disadvantages in terms of smoothness, manufacturing cost and shape characteristics. These advantages and disadvantages make them more suitable for certain vehicles.

The combustion chamber is the area where compression and combustion take place. As the piston moves from BDC to TDC, you can see that the size of the combustion chamber changes. It has a maximum volume as well as a minimum volume. The difference between the maximum and the minimum is called the displacement and is measured in liter or CCs (Cubic Centimeters, where 1,000 cubic centimeters equals a liter). It varies with cylinder bore size, length of piston stroke, and number of cylinders. Engine displacement is calculated by multiplying the number of cylinders in the engine by the piston displacement of one cylinder. Most normal car engines fall somewhere between 1.5 liter (1,500 cc) and 4.0 liters (4,000 cc). If you have a 4-cylinder engine and each cylinder displaces half a liter, then the entire engine is a 2.0-liter engine. If each cylinder displaces half a liter and there are six cylinders arranged in a V-shaped configuration, you have a 3.0-liter V-6.

Generally, the displacement tells you something about how much power an engine can produce. A cylinder that displaces half a liter can hold twice as much fuel-air mixture as a cylinder that displaces a quarter of a liter, and therefore you would expect about twice as much power from the large cylinder (if everything else is equal). So a 2.0-liter engine is roughly half as powerful as a 4.0-liter engine. You can get more displacement in an engine either by increasing the number of cylinders or by making the combustion chambers of all the cylinders bigger (or both).

The piston displacement seems to be the same as the total cylinder volume, but it is not. Total cylinder volume is the sum of the piston displacement and the clearance volume. The clearance volume is the combustion chamber volume with the piston at TDC. Compression ratio is the total volume of a cylinder divided by its clearance volume. In theory, the higher the compression ratio, the greater the efficiency of the engine, and the more power an engine will produce on condition that it holds a given quantity of fuel. However, there are practical limits to how high a compression ratio can be. The high ratio leads to high combustion chamber temperature. It results in the formation of oxides of nitrogen, a primary air pollutant. In the early 1970s, the compression ratio is lowered to about 8 and low octane, low lead or unleaded fuel is used. Now, EFI engine can raise compression ratio to 9 and 10 to 1 range for good performance and economy.

In today's world, there has been a growing emphasis on the pollution due to exhaust emissions of engines. This has created new interest in alternate power sources and internal combustion engine refinements that were not economically feasible in prior years. Although a few limited-production battery-powered electric vehicles have appeared from time to time, they have not proved competitive owing to cost and operating characteristics. However, the gasoline engine, with its new emission-control devices to improve emission performance, has not yet been challenged significantly.

New Words

1. reciprocating ['rɪˈsɪprəˌkeɪtɪŋ] adj. 往复的,来回的
2. originally [əˈdʒɪnəlɪ] adv. 原来地,最初地
3. flexibility [ˌflɛksəˈbɪlətɪ] n. 灵活性,适应性,机动性
4. stroke [stroʊk] n. 行程,冲程
5. cycle [ˈsaɪkəl] n. 循环
6. intake [ˈɪnˌtek] n. 入口,进口
7. exhaust [ɪɡˈzɔst] n. 排气,排气装置
8. figure [ˈfɪɡjər] n. 图形,图像
9. revolve [rɪˈvɑːlv] v. 旋转
10. valve [vælv] n. 阀门
11. vaporize [ˈvepəˌraɪz] vt./vi. (使)蒸发
12. carburetor [ˈkɑːbəˌreɪtə] n. 化油器
13. explode [ɪkˈsploʊd] v. 爆炸
14. introduce [ˌɪntrəˈduːs] vt. 引进,引导
15. linear [ˈlɪnɪər] adj. 线的,成直线的
16. anyway [ˈɛnɪˌwe] adv. 不管怎样
17. core [kɔr] n. 核心
18. lawn [lɔn] n. 草坪
19. mower [ˈmoʊə(r)] n. 割草机
20. arrange [əˈrendʒ] v. 排列,安排
21. horizontal [ˌhɔrəˈzɑntl] adj. 水平的
22. oppose [əˈpoʊz] v. 反对,使对立
23. bank [bæŋk] n. 一系列,一排
24. inclination [ˌɪnˌklɪˈneɪʃən] n. 倾斜,斜度
25. degree [dɪˈɡri] n. 度
26. configuration [kənˌfɪɡjəˈreɪʃn] n. 轮廓,结构
27. smoothness [ˈsmuðnɪs] n. 平滑,平坦
28. cubic [ˈkjubɪk] adj. 立方的
29. centimeter [ˈsɛntəˌmitə] n. 厘米
30. liter [ˈlitə] n. 升
31. displacement [dɪsˈplesmənt] n. 位移,排量
32. multiply [ˈmʌltəˌplaɪ] v. 乘,增加
33. quarter [ˈkwɔːrtə(r)] n. 一刻钟,四分之一
34. calculate [ˈkælkjəˌlet] v. 计算
35. clearance [ˈklɪrəns] n. 间隔,距离
36. quantity [ˈkwɑntəti] n. 数量
37. lead [liːd] n. 铅
38. oxide [ˈɑːksaɪd] n. 氧化物
39. nitrogen [ˈnaɪtrədʒən] n. [化]氮
40. lower [ˈloʊə(r)] v. 降低,减弱
41. performance [pərˈfɔːrməns] n. 性能
42. significantly [sɪɡˈnɪfəkəntlɪ] adv. 意味深长地,值得注目地

Phrases and Expressions

1. mass production　大规模生产
2. four-stroke cycle engine　四冲程发动机
3. Otto cycle　奥托循环
4. intake stroke　进气行程
5. compression stroke　压缩行程
6. power stroke　做功行程
7. exhaust stroke　排气行程
8. Top Dead Center(TDC)　上止点
9. Bottom Dead Center(BDC)　下止点
10. intake valve　进气门
11. exhaust valve　排气门
12. combustion chamber　燃烧室
13. go up　上升,增长
14. spark plug　火花塞
15. in-line engine　直列式发动机
16. flat engine　对置式发动机
17. cylinder bore　汽缸内径
18. engine displacement　发动机排量
19. in theory　理论上
20. compression ratio　压缩比

Notes to Text

1. Reliability, compact size, and range of operation later became important factors.
后来,汽油机的可靠性、紧凑的尺寸以及宽泛的工作范围成为人们选用汽油机的重要因素。

2. The four-stroke approach is also known as the Otto cycle, in honor of Nikolaus Otto, who invented it in 1867.
尼古拉斯·奥托在1867发明了发动机的四冲程循环方式,为了纪念他,这种循环方式也被称为奥托循环。

3. When the mixture is compressed, not only does the pressure in the cylinder go up, but also the temperature increases.
当可燃混合物被压缩时,不但汽缸内的压力会上升,而且温度也会升高。

4. That is typical of most lawn mowers, but most cars have more than one cylinder (four, six and eight cylinders are common).
大多数割草机用的是典型的单缸发动机。但是,大多数汽车的发动机不止一个汽缸(常见的是四缸、六缸和八缸)。

5. The V-type engine has two banks of cylinders which have an inclination of 60 to 90 degrees.
V型发动机有两排汽缸,这两排汽缸相互倾斜成60°到90°角。

6. Engine displacement is calculated by multiplying the number of cylinders in the engine by the piston displacement of one cylinder.
发动机的排量是用汽缸数乘以一个汽缸的活塞位移的乘积(汽缸的工作容积)而得到的。

7. The compression ratios of most gasoline engines are restricted within the limit of 11.5 to 1.

大多数发动机的压缩比被限制在了 11.5∶1 的范围内。

Exercises

1. Answer the following questions to the text.

(1) List the four strokes of a four-stroke engine in proper order, please.

(2) How many ways the cylinders are arranged in a multi-cylinder engine? What are they?

(3) How is the engine displacement calculated?

(4) What is the total cylinder volume?

(5) Why is compression ratio of the engine controlled?

2. Translate the following phrases and expressions into Chinese.

(1) cylinder bore

(2) lawn mower

(3) combustion chamber

(4) exhaust stroke

(5) engine displacement

(6) in-line engine

3. Translate the following sentences into Chinese.

(1) The reciprocating-piston internal combustion system has been the most successful for automobiles, while diesel engines are widely used for trucks and buses.

(2) The four-stroke approach is also known as the Otto cycle, in honor of Nikolaus Otto, who invented it in 1867. The four strokes are intake stroke, compression stroke, power stroke, exhaust stroke.

(3) Finally, once the piston hits near the BDC, the exhaust valve opens. Then the piston again moves up in the cylinder and the burned gas are pushed out.

(4) Different configurations have different advantages and disadvantages in terms of smoothness, manufacturing-cost and shape characteristics.

(5) Engine displacement is calculated by multiplying the number of cylinders in the engine by the piston displacement of one cylinder.

(6) In theory, the higher the compression ratio, the greater the efficiency of the engine, and the more power an engine will produce on condition that it holds a given quantity of fuel.

Part III Listening and Speaking

SWOT Analysis A

A—Manager A   B—Manager B

A: We are meeting today to make a SWOT analysis for our company, based on our performance over the last years. Just to remind you, SWOT stands for strengths, weaknesses, opportunities and threats. Let's start right from the top. What do you think about our strengths?

B: I think our main competitive advantage is the strength of our marketing team and advertising. We've been able to have a great deal of market penetration and have established a strong presence in the market, both in sales and in identity.

A: I agree. We've put a lot of emphasis on market development. That leads directly to our weakness, I think, because we have focused heavily on marketing, we have not made much leeway in product development. To keep our reputation with consumers, we need to put more effort into product quality, especially in performance and safety.

B: Well, let's talk about opportunities, shall we? I think that by focusing on improving our weakness and coming up with the reliability and stability of our cars, we can reach even more of a consumer base than we are now. Because of our status in the market, if we boosted our new model product development, we could dominate the market.

A: So what about our threats? Are there any strong competitors out there?

B: Yes. Nowadays, we're in a very competitive environment. Because of the great potential of our market, competitors come from both at home and abroad. The foreign companies have the advantage of better technology, while the domestic companies, such as BYD, China Automobile, etc, are competitive at price.

A: With competition this intense, we've got to find a way to outsmart the other guys. We should try to develop more competitive products both in quality and in price.

SWOT Analysis B

A—Manager A   B—Manager B

A: Do you agree with the SWOT that came out of our annual review meeting?

B: I agree with parts of it, but I just don't think the evaluation of current opportunities is realistic or even viable.

A: What do you mean? The report said we could boost our sales by addressing international distribution problems. Don't you think that would work?

B: No, I agree solving problems with our import and export side would help to boost revenue, but I just don't think we could achieve as much as 50% or more, which is what the analysis yielded. The problems are more complex than the SWOT took into account.

A: Well, I'd like to know your opinion about this.

B: I believe that we should focus on domestic market. From the performance report over the last year, the sales at home count for 70%. While the domestic market becomes more and more potential in recent years. Therefore, it is our first priority to develop new products which cater for the needs of domestic market.

A: Do you at least agree with the threat analysis?

B: Yes, I think determining our competitors' strengths and weaknesses is much more straightforward. We can list our threats on one hand, there are Geely, Chery, and BYD, etc.

Part IV Reading Material

Different Types of Engines

We are familiar with two types of engines found in nearly every car and truck on the road today. They are gasoline and diesel engines. Both are classified as four-stoke reciprocating internal-combustion engines and two-stroke engines. Two-stroke engines are commonly found in lower-power applications such as jet skis. Two-stroke engines have three important advantages over four-stroke engines:

Two-stroke engines do not have valves, which simplify their construction and lower their weight.

Two-stroke engines fire once every revolution, while four-stroke engines fire once every other revolution. This gives two-stroke engines a significant power boost.

Two-stroke engines can work in any orientation. A standard four-stroke engine may have problems with oil flow unless it is upright, and solving this problem can add complexity to the engine.

These advantages make two-stroke engines lighter, simpler and less expensive to manufacture. Two-stroke engines also have the potential to pack about twice the power into the same space because there are twice as many power strokes per revolution. The combination of light weight and twice the power gives two-stroke engines a great power-to-weight ratio compared to many four-stroke engine designs.

Start with the point where the spark plug fires. Fuel and air in the cylinder have been compressed, and when the spark plug fires the mixture, the resulting explosion drives the piston downward. Notes that as the piston moves downward, it is compressing the air-fuel mixture in the crankcase. As the piston approaches the bottom of its stroke, the exhaust port is uncovered. The pressure in the cylinder drives most of the exhaust gases out of cylinder. As the piston finally bottoms out, the intake port is uncovered. The piston's movement has pressurized the mixture in the crankcase, so it rushes into the cylinder, displacing the remaining exhaust gases and filling the cylinder with a fresh charge of fuel. Notes that in many two-stroke engines that use a cross-flow design, the piston is shaped so that the incoming fuel mixture doesn't simply flow right over the top of the piston and out the exhaust port. Now the momentum in the crankshaft starts driving the piston back toward the spark plug for the compression stroke. As the air-fuel mixture in the piston is compressed, a vacuum is created in the crankcase. This vacuum opens the reed valve and sucks air-fuel mixture from the carburetor.

Once the piston moves up to the end of the compression stroke, the spark plug fires again to repeat the cycle. It's called a two-stroke engine because there is a compression stroke and then a combustion stroke. In a four-stroke engine, there are separate intake, compression, combustion and exhaust strokes. You can see that the piston is really doing three different things in a two-stroke engine:

On one side of the piston is the combustion chamber, where the piston is compressing the air-fuel mixture and capturing the energy released by the ignition of the fuel.

On the other side of the piston is the crankcase, where the piston is creating a vacuum to suck in air-fuel mixture from the carburetor through the reed valve and then pressurizing the crankcase so that air-fuel mixture is forced into the combustion chamber.

Meanwhile, the sides of the piston are acting like valves, covering and uncovering the intake and exhaust ports drilled into the sides of the cylinder wall.

You can now see that two-stroke engines have two important advantages over four-stroke engines: they are simpler and lighter, and they produce about twice as much power. But why do cars and trucks use four-stroke engines? There are four main reasons.

Two-stroke engines don't last nearly as long as four-stroke engines. The lack of a dedicated lubrication system means that the parts of a two-stroke engine wear a lot faster.

Two-stroke oil is expensive, and you need about 4 ounces of it per gallon of gas. You would burn about a gallon of oil every 1,000 miles if you used a two-stroke engine in a car.

Two-stroke engines do not use fuel efficiently, so you would get fewer miles per gallon.

Two-stroke engines produce a lot of pollution. The pollution comes from two sources. The first is the combustion of the oil. The oil makes all two-stroke engines smoky to some extent, and a badly worn two-stroke engine can emit huge clouds of oily smoke. The second is that each time a new charge of air-fuel is loaded into the combustion chamber, part of it leaks out through the exhaust port. That's why you see a sheet of oil around any two-stroke boat motor. The combination of the leaking hydrocarbons from the fresh fuel and the leaking oil is a real mess for the environment.

These disadvantages mean that two-stoke engines are used only in applications where the motor is not used very often and a fantastic power-to-weight ratio is important.

Unit 3 Crank Connecting Rod Mechanism and Body Group

Part Ⅰ Illustrated English

Diagram of Crank Connecting Rod Mechanism and Body Group

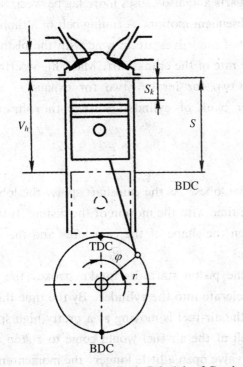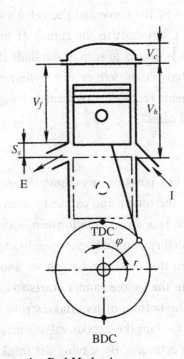

Fig. 3-1 Basic Principle of Crank Connecting Rod Mechanism

TDC—top dead center 上止点
BDC—bottom dead center 下止点
E—exhaust port 排气口
I—intake port 进气口
S—piston stroke 活塞行程
S_k—piston clearance from TDC 活塞离上止点距离
S_s—port height 孔口高度
r—crank radius 曲柄半径
φ—crank angle 曲柄角
V_f—charge volume 每缸充气体积(二冲程)
V_h—swept volume of a cylinder 气缸工作体积,每缸排量
V_c—combustion chamber volume 燃烧室容积
$V_c + V_h$—cylinder total volume 气缸总容积
$(V_c + V_h)/V_c$—compression ratio 压缩比

Part II Technical and Practical Reading

Valve Train

The valve train consists of the valves and a mechanism that opens and closes them. The opening and closing system is called a camshaft. The camshaft has lobes on it that move the valves up and down. Most modern engines have the overhead camshaft. This means that the camshaft is located above the valves. The cams on the shaft activate the valves directly or through a very short linkage. Older engines used a camshaft located in the sump near the crankshaft. Rods linked the cam below to valve lifters above the valves. This approach has more moving parts and also causes more lag between the cam's activation of the valve and the valve's subsequent motion. A timing belt or a timing chain links the crankshaft to the camshaft so that the valves are in sync with the pistons. The camshaft is geared to turn at one-half the rate of the crankshaft. Many high-performance engines have four valves per cylinder (two for intake, two for exhaust), and this arrangement requires two camshafts per bank of cylinders, hence the phrase "dual overhead cams".

Lobes

The key parts of any camshaft are the lobes. As the camshaft spins, the lobes open and close the intake and exhaust valves in time with the motion of the piston. It turns out that there is a direct relationship between the shape of the cam lobes and the way the engine performs in different speed ranges.

When the intake valve opens and the piston starts its intake stroke, the air-fuel mixture in the intake runner starts to accelerate into the cylinder. By the time the piston reaches the bottom of its intake stroke, the air-fuel is moving at a pretty high speed. If we were to slam the intake valve shut, all of the air-fuel would come to a stop and not enter the cylinder. By leaving the intake valve open a little longer, the momentum of the fast-moving air-fuel continues to force the air-fuel into the cylinder as the piston starts its compression stroke. So the faster the engine goes, the faster the air-fuel moves, and the longer we want the intake valve to stay open. We also want the valve to open wider at higher speeds. And this parameter, called valve lift, is governed by the cam lobe profile.

Any given camshaft will be perfect only at one engine speed. At every other engine speed, the engine won't perform to its potential. A fixed camshaft is, therefore, always a compromise. This is why carmakers have developed schemes to vary the cam profile as the engine speed changes.

Camshaft Arrangements

There are several different arrangements of camshafts on engines. The most common types contain the Single Overhead Cam (SOHC) engine, the Double Overhead Cam (DOHC) engine, the pushrod engine.

Single Overhead Cams

This arrangement denotes an engine with one cam per head. So if it is an in-line 4-cylinder or in-line 6-cylinder engine, it will have one cam; if it is a V-6 or V-8, it will have two cams (one for each head). The cam actuates rocker arms that press down on the valves, opening them. Springs return the valves to their closed position. These springs have to be very strong, because at a high engine speed, the valves are pushed down very quickly, and it is the springs that keep the valves in contact with the rocker arms. If the springs were not strong enough, the valves might come away from the rocker arms and snap back. This is an undesirable situation that would result in extra wear on the cams and rocker arms.

Double Overhead Cam

A double overhead cam engine has two cams per head. So in-line engines have two cams, and V-type engines have four. Usually, double overhead cams are used on engines with four or more valves per cylinder. However, a single camshaft simply cannot fit enough cam lobes to actuate all of those valves.

The main reason to use double overhead cams is to allow for more intake and exhaust valves. More valves mean that intake and exhaust gases can flow more freely, because there are more openings for them to flow through. This increases the power of the engine.

On single and double overhead cam engines, the cams are driven by the crankshaft, via either a belt or a chain called the timing belt or the timing chain. These belts and chains need to be replaced or adjusted at regular intervals. If a timing belt breaks, the cam will stop spinning and the piston could hit the open valves.

Pushrod Engines

Like SOHC and DOHC engines, the valves in a pushrod engine are located in the head, above the cylinder. The key difference is that the camshaft on a pushrod engine is inside the engine block, rather than in the head.

The cam actuates long rods that go up through the block and into the head to move the rockers. These long rods add mass to the system, which increases the load on the valve springs. This can limit the speed of pushrod engines; the overhead camshaft, which eliminates the pushrod from the system, is one of the engine technologies that made higher engine speed possible.

The camshaft in a pushrod engine is often driven by gears or a short chain. Gear-drives are generally less prone to breakage than belt-drives, which are often found in overhead cam engines.

Variable Valve Timing

  There are a couple of novel ways by which carmakers vary the valve timing. One system used on some Honda engines is called Variable Valve Timing and Lift Electronic Control (VTEC). VTEC is an electronic and mechanical system in some Honda engines that allows the engine to have multiple camshafts. VTEC engines have an extra intake cam with its own rocker, which follows this cam. The profile on this cam keeps the intake valve open longer than the other cam profile. At low engine speeds, this rocker is not connected to any valves. At high engine speeds, a piston locks the extra rocker to the two rockers that control the two intake valves.

  Some cars use a device that can advance the valve timing. This does not keep the valves open longer; instead, it opens them later and closes them later. This is done by rotating the camshaft ahead a few degrees. If the intake valves normally open at 10 degrees before Top Dead Center (TDC) and close at 190 degrees after TDC, the total duration is 200 degrees. The opening and closing time can be shifted using a mechanism that rotates the cam ahead a little as it spins. So the valve might open at 10 degrees after TDC and close at 210 degrees after TDC. Closing the valve 20 degrees later is good, but it would be better to be able to increase the duration that the intake valve is open.

  Several engine manufacturers are experimenting with systems that would allow infinite variability in valve timing. For example, imagine that each valve had a solenoid on it that could open and close the valve using computer control rather than relying on a camshaft. With this type of system, you would get best engine performance. Something will be looked forward to in the future.

New Words

1. mechanism ['mekə,nızəm] n. 机械装置
2. camshaft ['kæmʃæft] n. 凸轮轴
3. lobe [loub] n. 突出部, 凸角
4. cam [kæm] n. 凸轮
5. linkage ['lıŋkıdʒ] n. 连接, 连合
6. sump [sʌmp] n. 油底壳
7. rod [rɑːd] n. 杆, 棒
8. lifter ['lıftɚ] n. (气门)挺杆
9. subsequent ['sʌbsı,kwənt] adj. 后来的
10. lag [læg] n. 延迟, 落后
11. timing ['taımıŋ] v. 正时, 计时
12. belt [belt] n. 传动带, (机器)皮带
13. chain [tʃen] n. 链子
14. gear [gır] v. (使)适合 n. 齿轮
15. spin [spın] v. 快速旋转; 回旋
16. bottom ['bɑːtəm] n. 底部
17. slam [slæm] v. 猛推
18. profile ['proufaıl] n. 外形, 轮廓
19. scheme [skim] n. 计划, 配置; 体制
20. actuate ['æktʃu,et] vt. 驱使
21. press [pres] v. 挤压
22. spring [sprıŋ] n. 弹簧
23. interval ['ıntərvl] n. 间隔
24. mass [mæs] n. (物)质量

25. load [loud] n. 负荷
26. prone [proun] adj. 易于……的；倾向于……的
27. duration [dju'reɪʃn] n. 持续时间
28. solenoid ['soulənɔɪd] n. 螺线管

Phrases and Expressions

1. valve train　配气机构
2. overhead camshaft　顶置式凸轮轴
3. valve lifter　气门挺杆
4. timing belt　正时皮带
5. timing chain　正时链条
6. valve lift　气门升程
7. cam lobe　凸轮的工作部分，凸轮的凸起部
8. Single Over Head Cam (SOHC) engine　顶置单凸轮轴发动机
9. Double Over Head Cam (DOHC) engine　顶置双凸轮轴发动机
10. pushrod engine　推杆发动机
11. rocker arm　摇臂
12. snap back　迅速跳回，很快恢复
13. cylinder head　汽缸盖
14. engine block　发动机汽缸体
15. valve spring　气门弹簧
16. Variable Valve Timing (VVT)　可变气门正时
17. valve timing　配气（相位）正时

Notes to Text

1. A timing belt or a timing chain links the crankshaft to the camshaft so that the valves are in sync with the pistons.
曲轴与凸轮轴通过正时皮带或正时链条连接起来，以便使气门与活塞同步。

2. The camshaft is geared to turn at one-half the rate of the crankshaft.
凸轮轴转动应与曲轴相配合，其速度是曲轴转速的一半。

3. As the camshaft spins, the lobes open and close the intake and exhaust valves in time with the motion of the piston.
当凸轮轴快速旋转时，凸角可随着活塞的运动及时地开启和关闭进、排气门。

4. It turns out that there is a direct relationship between the shape of the cam lobes and the way the engine performs in different speed ranges.
这证明了凸轮凸角的形状与发动机在不同速度范围内的工作情况有直接的关系。

5. These springs have to be very strong because at a high engine speed, the valves are pushed down very quickly, and it is the springs that keep the valves in contact with the rocker arms.
因为当发动机高速运转时，气门被非常快速地推下并且气门弹簧要让气门与摇臂保持接触，所以气门弹簧必须是强有力的。

Exercises

1. **Answer the following questions to the text.**

(1) Why the lobes are the key parts of automobiles?
(2) What is the Single Over Head Cam (SOHC) engine?
(3) What is the Double Over Head Cam (DOHC) engine?
(4) What is the pushrod engine?
(5) What is VTEC?

2. **Translate the following phrases and expressions into Chinese.**

(1) Single Over Head Cam (SOHC) engine
(2) Double Over Head Cam (DOHC) engine
(3) pushrod engine
(4) cam lobe
(5) Variable Valve Timing (VVT)
(6) engine block

3. **Translate the following sentences into Chinese.**

(1) The cams on the shaft activate the valves directly or through a very short linkage.

(2) This approach has more moving parts and also causes more lag between the cam's activation of the valve and the valve's subsequent motion.

(3) When the intake valve opens and the piston starts its intake stroke, the air-fuel mixture in the intake runner starts to accelerate into the cylinder.

(4) If the springs were not strong enough, the valves might come away from the rocker arms and snap back.

(5) However, a single camshaft simply cannot fit enough cam lobes to actuate all of those valves.

(6) VTEC engines have an extra intake cam with its own rocker, which follows this cam. The profile on this cam keeps the intake valve open longer than the other profile.

Part Ⅲ　Listening and Speaking

Market Research A

A—Sales Manager　B—General Manager

A: I went over the sales in the market research report. If you take that report and compare it with our survey of consumer buying habits, there's only one conclusion...

B: What's that?
A: It seems that this market is sensitive to price. So we need to be cautious of price.
B: So, should we start low?
A: I think that would be a good idea. Price is an important variable in our market, so we can use it to build out customer base. If our customers get hooked in the low introductory price, they will buy and become more loyal to our brand. Later on, when we hit a peak in sales and after our customer base is solid on our products, we can bring the price up.
B: That sounds like a really clever marketing strategy.
A: This is a very competitive market. We've got to come up with a few clever strategies in order to keep our place on top.
B: I think our main strength is with young consumers because of the fashion styled body, and the relatively high cost effectiveness of our cars.
A: That is who we are targeting. The young consumers are fast to commit, but fickle to stay with a brand. Our challenge is customer loyalty.

Market Research B

A—Mr. Thomas B—Mr. Zhang

A: Welcome to our company, Mr. Zhang.
B: Glad to have the opportunity of visiting your company and I hope to conclude some business with your company.
A: Could I have some information about your scope of business?
B: Yes, we mainly deal in automobiles and mechanical appliances, which we are in for quite some time. And as you know, our company has achieved great success in exporting cars in recent years.
A: That's just under our line of business.
B: Then you'll find something interesting.
A: May I have a look at your catalogue?
B: Here you are. This is a copy of catalogue, which will give you a good idea of the products we handle. Which model do you think might find a ready market at your end?
A: I prefer the economy with automatic transmission. If they are of high quality and prices are reasonable, we'll purchase large quantities of them. And as you know that because of the economic crisis, we are in a weak market. If you want to increase your sale, you will have to lower your price to some degree.
B: But that will make our profits go down. A good product will sell well whether the market is up or down — it creates its own market.
A: I know, but I think if you lower the price, and spend a little more money on quality analysis, sales will go up.

B: You mean we should increase market share while we are in a market slump. Then when market fluctuations stop, we can slowly raise the prices and make bigger profits.

A: Yes, you are quite right. By the way, could you provide some technical data? I'd like to know more about your products.

B: Of course. Compared to other competing products, this model has many advantages. The best feature of this model is that it is novel and fashionable in design. What's more, it operates at the touch of a button, so it's very flexible. And based on the market research we have done, we can forecast that the market for this model will increase rapidly over the next several years.

A: I hope this visit of mine will be the beginning of a long friendly cooperation between us.

B: I hope so, too.

Part IV   Reading Material

Crankshaft and Connecting Rod Mechanism

In a reciprocating engine, the power mechanism is called the crankshaft and connecting rod assembly. In this assembly, all of the major units such as the engine crankcase and cylinder block, the piston and connecting rod, and the crankshaft and flywheel work in close cooperation to convert thermal energy into mechanical energy used to drive the vehicle.

The engine crankcase and cylinder block are usually cast in one piece and therefore can be seen as the largest and most intricate piece of metal in automobile. Even when the cylinders, the cylinder heads, or cylinder sleeves are separate pieces, the crankcase is still the largest single part in the engine, to which all of the engine parts are attached directly or indirectly. The crankcase house, the crankshaft and, in most cases, the camshaft also. The cylinder block contains the pistons which are linked to the crankshaft by means of the connecting rods. The crankcase and cylinder block are usually made of high grade cast alloy iron to improve wear characteristics of the cylinders. This major unit must be strong and rigid enough to withstand any bending or distortion.

The piston consists of piston head, piston rings, piston lands, piston skirt, and piston pin hole. The piston head is the top surface against which the explosive force is exerted. It may be flat, concave, or convex. It may also be in any other shape to promote turbulence or help control combustion. The piston rings carried in the ring grooves are of two basic types: compression rings and oil-control rings. Both types are made in a wide variety of design.

The upper compression rings are used to prevent compression leakage; the lower oil-control rings are used to control the amount of oil being deposited on the cylinder wall. The piston lands are the parts of piston between the ring grooves. The lands provide a seating surface for the sides of the piston rings. The main section of a piston is known as the skirt. It forms a bearing area in contact with the cylinder wall. The piston pin hole in the piston also serves as a bearing for the piston pin, which is used to connect the connecting rod.

The crankshaft can change the reciprocating motion of the piston into rotary motion and handles the entire power output. The crankshaft is actually made up of various parts such as main bearing journal, rod journal, crank bearing, counterbalanced weight and flywheel end. The connecting rod links its large end to the rod journal of the crankshaft and its small end to the piston. The function of the rod is to pass the reciprocating power of the piston to the crankshaft. The crankshaft revolves in bearings located in the engine crankcase, but the number of bearings used usually depends on the number of cylinders in the engine, and the design of the engine. Mechanically, a crankshaft without special balanced weights would have severe vibration when revolving. So, in order to reduce or eliminate such vibration, the crankshaft must be balanced. In other words, it must be provided with counterbalanced weights that extend rapidly from the crankshaft centerline in the opposite direction of the crank arms. In that way, the forces acting on the crankshaft are balanced and vibration is reduced.

Unit 4 Ventilation System and Gas Exchange Process

Part Ⅰ Illustrated English

Diagram of Ventilation System's Structure

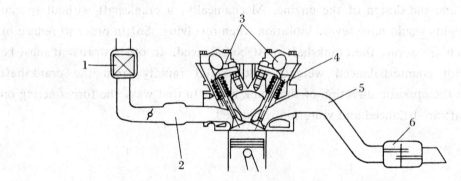

Fig. 4-1 The Structure of the Gas Exchange System

1. air filter 空气滤清器
2. intake pipe system 进气管系
3./4. air distribution mechanism 配气机构
5. exhaust pipe system 排气管系
6. muffler 消声器

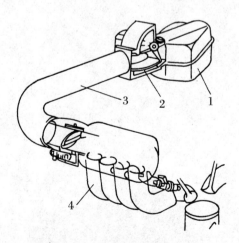

Fig. 4-2 Intake Pipe System

1. air filter 空气滤清器
2. air flow meter 空气流量计
3. inlet pipe assembly 进气管总成
4. inlet manifold 进气歧管

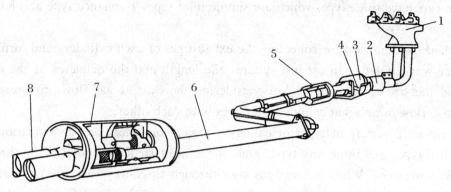

Fig. 4-3　Exhaust Pipe System

1. exhaust manifold　排气歧管
2. exhaust trunk　排气总管
3. catalytic converter　催化转化器
4. exhaust temperature sensor　排气温度传感器
5. deputy muffler　副消声器
6. rear exhaust pipe　后排气管
7. main muffler　主消声器
8. tail pipe　排气尾管

Part Ⅱ　Technical and Practical Reading

Structure of Ventilation System

If the engine is the heart of a car, the ventilation system of vehicles is the lung, which is responsible for providing quality, plenty of fresh air continuously, and is responsible for the waste gas discharging efficiently in a timely manner. This article will give an introduction around the gas exchange system and air distribution mechanism.

Gas Exchange System

In an internal combustion engine work cycle, the gas exchange system keeps fresh entering the combustion chamber, and taking the waste gas to the atmosphere after combustion, to ensure the continuous operation of the internal combustion engine. The gas exchange system includes air filter, intake manifold, exhaust pipe, exhaust muffler, three-way catalytic converter, exhaust gas recycling (EGR), turbo, etc.

Air filter is to filter the dust and impurities in the air, to feed clean air in the combustion chamber, to reduce the friction into the piston group and the valve group, the friction between piston and cylinder liner, and inhibition the intake noise of the engine. There are three types of air filter, inertial type, oil bath type, and filter type.

Air intake-tube is connected air filter to cylinder head tube. In gasoline engines, sometimes, the inlet pipe is the pipe between carburetor or electronic injection throttle and cylinder head. Air inlet pipe, especially the intake pipe of naturally aspirated high-speed vehicle, is very important to the fuel consumption, power, torque and emissions.

Modern cars have three types which are simple inlet pipe, resonance type and harmonic type.

Exhaust system used for collecting the exhaust gas of each cylinder, and turn it into the three-way catalytic. In exhaust system, the length and the diameter of the exhaust pipe and the size of the muffler are considering the exhaust gas flow, to prevent the exhaust airflow of adjacent cylinder interferes with each other.

There are a variety of types of exhaust purifier converters such as oxidation type, double bed type, and three-way type. One of the most frequently used is the three-way catalytic converters. When exhaust gas goes through three-way catalytic converters, it converts three main harmful substances in the waste gas (CH, CO, NO_x) into a harmless substance (H_2O, CO_2) high efficiency. Three-way catalytic converters shell with high temperature resistant stainless steel, coated with catalyst on internal honeycomb channels. When the waste gas through the purifier channel, carbon monoxide and hydrocarbons are oxidized by the oxygen of the air under the action of a catalyst, and then produce harmless water and carbon dioxide. The nitrogen oxides are returned to harmless oxygen and nitrogen.

Waste gas enters the muffler after purifier. Muffler is welded with sheet steel, installed in the centre or at the back of the exhaust system. There is a set of clapboard, chamber, holes and pipes inside it. Using the principle of sound wave reflection interference offsets each other to weak sound energy gradually. Thereby isolation and attenuation the exhaust noise. At present, more and more of the muffler adopts aluminum-coated stainless steel material which can reduce weight and prolong life.

EGR is mainly used to purify NO_x. Let part of the exhaust gas (5%~20%) enter the inlet pipe to the cylinder. The H_2O and CO_2 in exhaust gas increase mixture heat capacity, and then drop the combustion temperature. At last, the NO_x concentration in exhaust gas is reduced.

At present, the most commonly used type of crankcase ventilation is closed positive crankcase ventilation, which known as PCV. Fresh air from the air filter enters the crankcase and mixes with gas carry-over. Then the mixture is inhaled inlet pipe from the cylinder head cover after the measurement of metering valve. So there is just an amount of gas combustion again in the cylinder.

With cylinder volume and engine rotating speed constant, the engine power and fuel heat are directly proportional to the density of the fresh air in the cylinder. Therefore, before entering the cylinder, the engine power is increased by compressing the gas. On exhaust gas turbo chargers, the turbine is impacted at a certain direction by exhaust flow of high temperature, high pressure and high speed, result for high-speed rotation of the turbine. At last, the exhaust expel to atmosphere. Turbine and centrifugal compressor impeller is installed on the same shaft, so the fresh gas from the air filter is compressed by compressor impeller of high-speed rotation, and then the pressure of fresh gas rapid growth. Finally got in the diffuse, increasing the pressure and airflow velocity quickly before enter the cylinder. It increases the charging efficiency effectively.

Air Distribution Mechanism

Valve-train engine is used to open and close the inlet and exhaust valves of each cylinder according to the work cycle and ignition sequence in each cylinder timely, so to make the fresh gas enter the cylinder and exhaust discharge from the cylinder timely, in compression and power stroke, shut off the valve to make sure the sealing of the combustion chamber. There are valves overhead, in mid-place and at the back according to the camshaft arrangement, while there are valves overhead and special side depending on the valve location. All kinds of distribution mechanism can be divided into valve group and valve transmission. Valve transmission mainly includes the camshaft, timing gear, lifter, guide rod, push rod, rocker arm and rocker arm shaft, etc. Its role is to ensure the timely opening and closing of the valve and adequate opening according to the distribution phase.

The valve consists of valve head and valve stem. The temperature of the valve head is very high ($570 \sim 670$ K of the inlet valve, $1,050 \sim 1,200$ K of exhaust valve). It needs to bear the pressure of the gas, valve spring force and the inertial force of transmission components. With its scanty lubrication, cooling condition, the valve must have a certain strength, rigidity, heat resistance and wear resistance. Inlet valve is generally made from alloy steel (chrome steel, nickel chromium steel) while the exhaust valve from heat-resisting alloy (silicon chromium steel).

Valve seat can be directly bored on cylinder head or cylinder body, also can be made with good material separately, and then embedded into the cylinder head or cylinder body. It ensures the sealing of cylinder joins with the valve head and the conduction of the heat from the valve head.

The valve guide is used to ensure the linear motion of the valve. Make the valve and valve seat fit properly. In addition, the valve guide also has a role of heat conduction between the valve rod and the cylinder body.

The function of the valve spring is overcome the inertia force of the valve and transmission in the process of valve closing, to ensure valve located timely and prevent undermining its sealing when the engine vibration.

Camshaft is the key part of valve-train. It controls the distribution phase, and also be used to drive the oil pump, gasoline pumps and distributor in some motor. Camshaft is generally forged with high-quality steel; it can be cast with alloy iron or ductile iron, too. The work surface of the cam is generally fine grinding after heat treatment, to improve the wear resistance.

The function of the valve lifter is to transmit the thrust of the cam to push rod (or valve rod) and to bear the lateral force imposed by the camshaft rotation. Hydraulic lifter will introduce part of the oil to the hydraulic cylinder of the lifter. With the use of hydraulic lifter, it does not have to stay valve clearance for the compressible of the liquid, but can ensure the sealing when the valve heated expands.

The function of the push rod is transmitting the force from the column to rocker arm. Superior stiffness is required because it is the most flexible in the valve trains. The push rod should be shorter in the engine of the dynamic load.

Rocker arm and rocker arm shaft just like a lever actually, which used to apply the force from the push rod on the valve rod end to open the valve after changing direction. The rocker arm ratio is about 1.2~1.8. The long arm connects to the valve end, and the opposite side connects to the push rod.

New Words

1. ventilation [ˌventl'eʃn] n. 通风设备;空气流通
2. combustion [kəm'bʌstʃ(ə)n] n. 燃烧,氧化
3. chamber ['tʃeɪmbə] n. 室,腔
4. manifold ['mænɪfoʊld] n. 歧管, 支管
5. exhaust [ɪg'zɔst] n. 排气,废气
6. muffler ['mʌflə] n. 消音器
7. inertia [ɪ'nɜːʃə] n. 惯性,惰性,迟钝
8. throttle ['θrɑːtl] n. 节气门
9. resonance ['rezənəns] n. 共振,共鸣
10. harmonic [hɑːr'mɑːnɪk] n. 谐波,和声
11. emissions [ɪ'mɪʃnz] n. 排放
12. attenuation [əˌtenjuː'eɪʃn] adj. 衰减;变薄;稀释
13. atmosphere ['ætməsfɪr] n. 大气
14. interfere [ˌɪntər'fɪr] v. 冲击,冲突,干涉
15. oxidation [ˌɑksɪ'deʃən] n. 氧化
16. substance ['sʌbstəns] n. 物质,实质
17. catalyst ['kætlɪst] n. 催化剂;刺激因素
18. monoxide [mə'nɑkˌsaɪd] n. 一氧化物
19. turbine ['tɜːrbaɪn] n. 涡轮,涡轮机
20. diffuser [dɪ'fjuzɚ] n. 扩散器
21. impeller [ɪm'pelə] n. 叶轮
22. turbo ['tɜːboʊ] n. 涡轮增压
23. density ['dɛnsɪti] n. 密度
24. automatic [ˌɔtə'mætɪk] adj. 自动的,无意的,必然的
25. status ['stetəs] n. 地位,状态
26. crankcase ['kræŋkˌkeɪs] n. 曲轴箱
27. sequence ['sikwəns] n. 顺序,序列
28. sealing ['silɪŋ] n. 密封性
29. camshaft ['kæmʃæft] n. 凸轮轴
30. assemble [ə'sɛmbəl] v. 装配,总成
31. guarantee [ˌgærən'ti] vt. 保证,担保
32. prolong [prə'lɔːŋ] vt. 延长,拖长
33. interference [ˌɪntər'fɪrəns] n. 干扰,冲突;干涉
34. linear ['lɪniər] adj. 直线的
35. clearance ['klɪrəns] n. 间隙
36. lifter ['lɪftə] n. 挺柱
37. ductile ['dʌktəl] adj. 柔软的
38. thrust [θrʌst] n. 推力
39. hydraulic [haɪ'drɔlɪk] adj. 液力的

Phrases and Expressions

1. gas exchange system　进排气系统
2. air distribution mechanism　配气机构
3. intake manifold　进气歧管
4. exhaust pipe　排气管
5. exhaust muffler　排气消音器
6. three-way catalytic converter　三元催化转换器
7. exhaust gas recycling　废气再循环系统
8. fuel consumption　耗油量
9. air filter　空气滤清器
10. harmful substance　有害物质
11. ductile iron　球墨铸铁
12. heat treatment　耐热性能
13. wear resistance　耐磨性能
14. valve clearance　气门间隙
15. ignition sequence　点火顺序
16. valve guide　气门导管
17. valve seat　气门座
18. valve springs　气门弹簧
19. valve rotating mechanism　气门旋转机构
20. timing gear　正时齿轮
21. hydraulic lifter　液力挺柱
22. push rod　推杆
23. rocker arm (shaft)　摇臂(轴)
24. (inlet) exhaust advance angle　(进)排气提前角
25. (inlet) exhaust relay angle　(进)排气延迟角
26. valve overlap angle　气门重叠角

Notes to Text

1. If the engine is the heart of a car, the ventilation system of vehicles is the lung, which are responsible for providing quality, plenty of fresh air continuously, and is responsible for the waste gas discharging efficiently in a timely manner.

　　如果说发动机是汽车的心脏,那么汽车的通风系统就是汽车的肺。它负责连续不断地并以一定的时间间隔给发动机提供优质、足量的新鲜气体,并将废气及时、高效地排出。

2. Automobile exhaust system is an important complement of emissions and noise reduction. It is mainly composed of the exhaust pipe, exhaust muffler, three-way catalytic and tail pipe. Main function is to collect, clean, and sound attenuation the waste gas which made of combustion process and then led to the atmosphere.

　　汽车的排气系统是排放和降噪的重要总成。它主要由排气管、催化式净化器、消声器、尾管等组成。其主要功能是把发动机在燃烧过程中产生的废气从多个气缸内收集、清洁、消声,然后排入到大气中。

3. One of the most frequently used is the three-way catalytic converters. When exhaust gas go through three-way catalytic converters, it converts three main harmful substances in the waste gas (CH, CO, NO_x) into a harmless substance (H_2O, CO_2) high efficiency.

　　最常用的是三元型催化式净化器。它是一种在废气通过它时,能将其中的三种主要有害物质(碳氢化合物、一氧化碳、氮氧化合物)转化为无害物质(水、二氧化碳)的高效率净化器。

4. Let part of the exhaust gas (5%～20%) enter the inlet pipe to the cylinder. The H_2O and CO_2 in exhaust gas increase mixture heat capacity, and then drop the combustion temperature. At last, the NO_x concentration in exhaust gas is reduced.

引入废气中的一部分(5%～20%)进入进气管并到达气缸。废气中的水、二氧化碳可以使混合气热容量提高,从而使燃烧最高温度下降,氮氧化合物排出浓度减少。

5. With cylinder volume and engine rotating speed constant, the engine power and fuel heat are directly proportional to the density of the fresh air in the cylinder.

在气缸容积和内燃机转速不变的条件下,内燃机的功率与转化燃料热能的多少与供入气缸内新鲜气体的密度成正比。

6. Valve-train engine is used to open and close the inlet and exhaust valves of each cylinder according to the work cycle and ignition sequence in each cylinder timely, so to make the fresh gas enter the cylinder and exhaust discharge from the cylinder timely.

配气机构是按照发动机每一气缸内所进行的工作循环和点火顺序的要求,定时开启和关闭各气缸的进、排气门,使新鲜气体得以及时进入气缸,废气得以及时从气缸排出。

7. Valve transmission mainly includes the camshaft, timing gear, lifter, guide rod, push rod, rocker arm and rocker arm shaft, etc.

气门传动组主要包括凸轮轴、正时齿轮、挺柱、导杆、推杆、摇臂和摇臂轴等。

8. Its role is to ensure the timely open and close of the valve and adequate opening according to the distribution phase.

它的作用是使进、排气门按配气相位规定的时刻进行开闭,并保证有足够的开度。

Exercises

1. Answer the following questions to the text.

(1) What is the function of the valve guide?

(2) What is the air distribution mechanism composed of?

(3) What do EDR and PCV mean?

(4) What is the advantage of Hydraulic lifter?

(5) What are the requirements of the valve group?

2. Translate the following phrases and expressions into Chinese.

(1) exhaust muffler

(2) three-way catalytic converter

(3) exhaust gas recycling

(4) fuel consumption

(5) air filter

(6) valve clearance

(7) valve seat

(8) valve rotating mechanism

(9) timing gear

3. Translate the following sentences into Chinese.

(1) Air inlet pipe, especially the intake pipe of naturally aspirated high-speed vehicle, is very important to the fuel consumption, power, torque and emissions.

(2) Metering valve can adjust the mount of gas carry-over who is inhaled in cylinder according to the engine running status automatically.

(3) Valve seat can be directly bored on cylinder head or cylinder body, also can be made with good material separately.

(4) The function of the valve spring is overcome the inertia force of the valve and transmission in the process of valve closing.

(5) With the use of hydraulic lifter, it does not have to stay valve clearance for the compressible of the liquid, but can ensure the sealing when the valve heated expands.

(6) The rocker arm ratio is about 1.2~1.8. The long arm connects to the valve end, and the opposite side connects to the push.

Part Ⅲ　Listening and Speaking

Automotive Design A

A—Nick　B—Richard

A: Hello! What are you reading?
B: I'm reading a book about automobile.
A: May I have a look?
B: Sure. Here you are.
A: Ah! There are so many colorful car pictures in it. I guess the book must be very interesting and informative.
B: Yes, of course! The book tells me a lot about automobile in both structure and design. That will help me a lot in my work.
A: I am also very interested in automobile. Would you please tell me something about automobile structure and design?
B: OK. The automobile was invented one hundred years ago, but since then the design of the automobile has been changed so much that the cars on the streets have a great variety of styles and designs.
A: That's true. Cars are different in style and design because they are made by different manufactures.
B: You are right. But, have you ever noticed anything common about the automobiles running on streets?
A: Yes. Every automobile has a steering wheel, headlights, wheels, etc. But these are

the essential components of any automobiles.

B: You are right, but not very complete, I think. You know, automobiles are, indeed, quite different in design, but no matter how different, automobiles are basically similar in structure. To be exact, an automobile is composed of four sections such as automobile engine, chassis, body and electrical system.

A: Oh, I see. Could you please tell me how each section functions in an automobile?

B: All right. To my knowledge, the engine serves to supply power for driving automobile; the chassis acts as a support frame to assemble all the automobile components on it.

A: How about the other two sections?

B: The automobile body rests on the chassis and usually consists of a driving room, a loading or passenger room and possibly a trunk. The electrical system works to supply electric power for engine ignition, lighting, etc.

A: Oh, I see. I have learned a great deal from our talk. Thank you very much. By the way, may I borrow this book from you?

B: Sure.

Automotive Design B

A—Journalist   B—Product Manager

A: Your company is one of the leading companies in the automotive industry. And recently, your company has just launched a new model in the market. Can you introduce it briefly?

B: The Audi R8 combines Le Mans-winning technology, all-wheel drive, luxurious driving comfort and incredible performance. This is supposed to be the hit product of our company this year.

A: It sounds fantastic. By building mostly sedans, coupes and SUV, Audi earned a reputation for luxury touring cars. What we want to know is outstanding points that R8 owns.

B: Well. At first glance, it looks like an exotic Italian racer, but the Audi R8 is born and built in Germany. The R8 is a road car modeled after a champion racing car. Most super-cars are thought of as being kind of temperamental, you know, somewhat unreliable, not comfortable, and noisy. Audi, using its technology, found a way to have the same on-track performance of those vehicles, but not get rid of the premium luxury that Audi's known for.

A: How can you handle this perfect balance in one car?

B: It has all of company's engineering innovations over the last three decades. We make progress through technology.

A: Can you explain it in a more specific way? What kind of new technology does the Audi R8 have?

B: We have, for example, the Audi aluminum space frame, the Quatrain drive train, and the FSI engine technology. All the three that were designed by Audi are combined in this R8. The R8's power is proudly displayed in the design of the car. Audi's first ever mid-engine sports car features a muscular V8 or V10 motor, all-wheel drive and an ultra-light aluminum space frame. The mid-engine design place the engine between the rear and the front axles, ensuring the engine weight is made available evenly on all the wheels.

A: We noticed that the engine is visible through a transparent bonnet.

B: Exactly, this is what we want to show. An engine is the heart of the automobile. Our two engines, the V8 and V10 engines, are true eye catchers. There is no reason for us to hide them from the driver. If you start this engine for the first time, you will smile. There is sound behind you, the feeling, the vibration. This is great.

Part IV   Reading Material

Air Exchange Process and Variable Valve Timing

Air Exchange Process

The opening time and opening duration of inlet and exhaust valve is expressed by the crankshaft angle in engine, and we call it timing. In a four-stroke engine, the inlet valve opens when the crank throws on the Top Dead Center (TDC) and closes when the crank throws on the Bottom Dead Center (BDC). While the exhaust valve opens when the crank throws on the BDC, and closes when the crank throws on the TDC. The intake valve and the exhaust valve keep opening about 180°. However, the engine air charge or exhaust can not keep up with the high speed of crankshaft, so that the engine power will decline. Therefore, it takes the method of extender inlet and exhaust time in modern engine. That is to say, the valve does not open and close just when the crank throw is at TDC or BDC, but early and delayed certain crankshaft angle. So in order to improve emission, we have to improve the dynamic performance of engine.

According to the timing phase diagram, the air exchange process can be described as follows: near the end of the power stoke, before the piston reaches the TDC, the exhaust valve opens. With high temperature and high pressure, the exhaust discharges the cylinder by itself. In exhaust stroke, as the piston moves from the BDC to TDC, the exhaust was pushed out. Near the end of the exhaust stroke, before the piston reaches the TDC, the angle of the crank rotates during the time from the inlet valve opening to the piston reaching the TDC is called intake advance angle which generally is $10° \sim 30°$. Inlet valve opens early, so when the piston reaches the TDC, the inlet valve has a certain opening, so it can quickly get bigger inlet channel section, and reduce air intake resistance. From the inlet valve opened to the exhaust valve closed, equal to the sum of inlet advance angle and exhaust lag angle. The overlap angle should be appropriate. It will be inadequate intake and endless exhaust if it is too small, while the exhaust gas will back flow and badly affect the suction of the fresh gas if it is too big. Piston movement from TDC to BDC, the fresh gas in the inlet pipe forced suction under negative pressure of the cylinder. Inertia intake (air intake delay angle): after the intake stroke, the intake valves keep opening for a period of time to continue inlet by inertia.

Variable Valve Timing

When the engine speed is changed, the effect of increasing the intake airflow and promoting the exhaust gas will be different in the delay angle. For example, when the engine is at low speed, the inertia of air flow is small, if the inlet delay angle is too large, the partial admission will be pushed out by the up moving piston, reducing the inflating volume, and the percent of residual gas in the cylinder will be increased. When the engine operates at a high speed, the inertia of air flow is enormous, if increasing inlet delay angle and valve overlap angle, the volume will increase and decrease the percent of residual gas, making the ventilation process of engine approach perfect. All in all, the valve timing of a four-stroke engine should be able to increase the inlet angle and valve overlap angle as the increasing of engine speed. If the valve lift can also be increased as the increasing of engine speed, it will be more conducive to obtaining good engine performance at a high speed.

Variable distribution technology, can be divided into two major categories of variable valve timing and variable valve lifting, some engine only matches variable valve timing, such as Toyota's Variable Valve Timing-intelligent (VVT-I) engine, and some of the engine only matches variable valve lifting, such as Honda VTEC, while some engine matches of variable valve timing and variable valve lifting at the same time, such as Toyota VVTL-I, Honda I-VTEC. So it will take the Toyota VVTL-I and Honda's I-VTEC valve-train as an example to introduce as follows:

VVT-I is the abbreviation of Toyota's variable valve timing-intelligent system, and the VVT-I system has been widely installed in the latest Toyota car engine. Toyota VVT-I system can continuously adjust valve timing, but can't adjust the valve lift.

I-VTEC is the abbreviation of Honda's intelligent variable valve timing system. According to the change of engine speed, the adjustment of valve timing and valve lifting is adjusted in real time. Its working principle is: when the engine is from low speed to high speed, the computer automatically to press the oil to the small turbine in the intake camshaft drive gear. In this way, under the action of pressure, the small turbine rotation a small angle relative to the gear shell, this makes the forward and backward rotation of the camshaft in the range of 60 degrees. Thus if we change the inlet time, then we will achieve the objective of continuous adjustment valve timing.

Unit 5 Supply and Combustion of Gasoline Engine Fuel

Part Ⅰ Illustrated English

Diagram of Gasoline Engine Fuel System

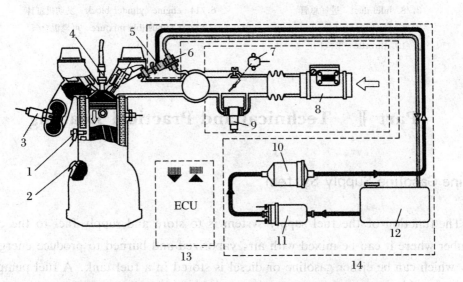

Fig. 5-1 The Basic Composition of Electronic Fuel Injection

1. knock transducer 爆震传感器
2. crankshaft position sensor 曲轴位置传感器
3. oxygen sensor 氧传感器
4. sparking plug 火花塞
5. fuel injector 喷油器
6. gas pressure regulator 汽油压力调节器
7. throttle position sensor 节气门位置传感器
8. air flow meter 空气流量计
9. idle speed regulator 怠速转速调节器
10. fuel filter 汽油滤清器
11. electric petrol pump 电动汽油泵
12. petrol tank 汽油箱
13. control system 控制系统
14. fuel supply system 燃油供给系统

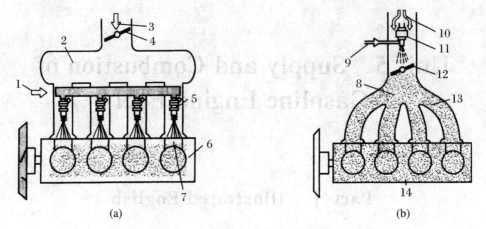

Fig. 5-2 Multi-point and Single Point Fuel Injection Systems
(a) Multi-point Fuel Injection System (MPI); (b) Single Point Fuel Injection System (SPI)

1./9. high pressure oil 高压油
2./8. inlet duct 进气总管
3./10. air 空气
4./12. throttle 节气门
5./11. fuel injector 喷油器
6./14. engine cylinder block 发动机缸体
7./13. combustible mixture 可燃混合气

Part II Technical and Practical Reading

Engine Gasoline Supply System

The function of the fuel supply system is to store and supply fuel to the cylinder chamber where it can be mixed with air, vaporized and burned to produce energy. The fuel, which can be either gasoline or diesel is stored in a fuel tank. A fuel pump draws the fuel from the tank through fuel lines and delivers it through a fuel filter to either a carburetor or a fuel injector, then delivered to the cylinder chamber for combustion.

In old cars, it is a carburetor that sends the correct air-fuel mixture to the engine. The carburetor is a mixing device which mixes liquid gasoline with air. The mixture must vary degree of richness continually to suit engine operation conditions. Therefore, electric fuel injection system has replaced the function of the carburetor in modern car engines.

Fuel injection system provides more exact air-fuel ratio control. Thus, engine develops better economy and emission control. Sensors read changes on the engine. A computer interprets the information and sends appropriate instruction to the engine's fuel controller. Then the injector sprays a measured amount of fuel down to the engine.

The term petrol injection is used to describe any system in which pressurized fuel is forced out of a nozzle in an atomized state to mix with a supply of air.

Modern systems are controlled electronically because this form of control enables the fuel quantity to be accurately set to suit the engine operating conditions. Strict emission control regulations have demanded precise metering of the fuel, although petrol injection systems are more expensive than carburetor fuel systems. They are now used to control the fuelling on all engines. Most petrol injection systems are integrated with the ignition system into an engine management system, including three basic subsystems. They are the fuel delivery system, air induction system, and the electronic control system.

Fuel Delivery System

The fuel delivery system consists of fuel tank, fuel pump, fuel filter, fuel delivery pipe (fuel rail), fuel injector, fuel pressure regulator, and fuel return pipe.

Fuel is delivered from the tank to the injector by means of an electric fuel pump. The pump is typically located in or near the fuel tank. Contaminants are filtered out by a high capacity in line fuel filter.

Fuel is maintained at a constant pressure by means of a fuel pressure regulator. Any fuel which is not delivered to the intake manifold by the injector is returned to the tank through a fuel return pipe.

The fuel delivery system is to supply the injectors with the fuel. Pressure is provided by an electric fuel pump. Some systems use two pumps: a low-pressure fuel pump that delivers fuel to the other, which develops the pressure.

Air Induction System

The air induction system consists of air cleaner, air flow meter, throttle valve, air intake chamber, intake manifold runner, and intake valve. When the throttle valve is open, air flows through the air cleaner, through the air flow meter (on L-type systems), past the throttle valve, and through a well-tuned intake manifold runner to the intake valve. Air delivered to the engine is a function of driver demand. As the throttle valve is opened further, more air is allowed to enter the engine cylinder.

Toyota engines use two different methods to measure intake air volume. L-type EFI system measures air flow directly by using an air flow meter. D-type EFI system measures air flow indirectly by monitoring the pressure in the intake manifold.

Electronic Control System

The electronic control system of an engine is mainly composed of ECU, sensors and actuators. Engine control computers are constructed using many different electronic circuits and components. Modern computers control many other engine systems in addition to the fuel injectors. The computer is usually located in a protected area away from engine vibration and heat, and is connected to the rest of the injection system by means of a sealed wiring harness plug. The computer receives signals from a number of sensors whenever the engine is running. From this input, the computer evaluates engine fuel needs and adjusts injector pulse width accordingly.

Operation

Air enters the engine through the air induction system where it is measured by the air flowmeter. As the air flows into the cylinder, fuel is mixed into the air by the fuel injector. Fuel injectors are arranged in the intake manifold behind each intake valve. The injectors are electrical solenoids which are operated by the ECU. The ECU pulses the injector by switching the injector ground circuit on and off. When the injector is turned on, it opens, spraying atomized fuel at the back side of the intake valve. As fuel is sprayed into the intake air stream, it mixes with the incoming air and vaporizes due to the low pressure in the intake manifold. The ECU signals the injector to deliver just enough fuel to achieve an ideal air-fuel ratio of 14.7:1, often referred to as stoichiometry. The precise amount of fuel delivered to the engine is a function of ECU control.

The ECU determines the basic injection quantity based upon measured intake air volume and engine RPM (revolutions per minute). Depending on engine operating conditions, injection quantity will vary. The ECU monitors variables such as coolant temperature, engine speed, throttle angle and exhaust oxygen content and makes injection corrections which determine final injection quantity.

Advantages of EFI

Uniform air-fuel mixture distribution: each cylinder has its own injector which delivers fuel directly to the intake valve. This eliminates the need for fuel to travel through the intake manifold, improving cylinder to cylinder distribution.

Highly accurate air-fuel ratio control throughout all engine operating conditions: EFI supplies a continuously accurate air-fuel ratio to the engine no matter what operating conditions are encountered. This provides better drive ability, fuel economy, and emissions control.

Superior throttle response and power: by delivering fuel directly at the back of the intake valve, the intake manifold design can be optimized to improve air velocity at the intake valve. This improves torque and throttle response.

Excellent fuel economy with improved emissions control: cold engine and wide open throttle enrichment can be reduced with an EFI engine, because fuel puddle in the intake manifold is not a problem. This results in better overall fuel economy and improved emissions control.

Improved cold engine start ability and operation: the combination of better fuel atomization and injection directly at the intake valve improves ability to start and run a cold engine.

Simpler mechanics, reduced adjustment sensitivity: the EFI system does not rely on any major adjustments for cold enrichment or fuel metering. Because the system is mechanically simple, maintenance requirements are reduced.

New Words

1. vaporize ['veɪpəˌraɪz] v. (使)蒸发,(使)汽化
2. carburetor ['kɑːbjʊretə] n. 汽化器,化油器
3. sensor ['sensə] n. 传感器,灵敏元件
4. appropriate [ə'prəʊprieit] adj. (适)恰当的
5. pressurize ['preʃəˌraɪz] v. 对……施加压力,给……增压
6. nozzle ['nɒzəl] n. 管嘴,喷嘴
7. injector [in'dʒektə] n. 喷油器
8. discharge [dis'tʃɑːdʒ] v. 执行,履行
9. spray [spreɪ] v. 喷
10. circuit ['səːkit] n. 电路,线路
11. vibration [vaɪ'breɪʃən] n. 颤动,振动
12. atomize ['ætəmaɪz] v. 使分裂为原子,将……喷成雾状

Phrases and Expressions

1. fuel supply system 燃油供给系统
2. fuel tank 燃油箱
3. fuel pump 燃油泵
4. fuel line 油管
5. fuel filter 燃油滤清器
6. fuel injector 燃油喷射器
7. cylinder chamber 气缸腔室
8. catalytic converter 催化转化器
9. degree of richness 浓度
10. air-fuel ratio 空燃比
11. fuel consumption 燃料消耗(量),耗油率
12. wiring harness 线束
13. electronic fuel injection (EFI) 电子燃油喷射
14. intake manifold 进气歧管
15. fuel delivery system 燃油供给系统
16. air induction system 进气系统
17. fuel pressure regulator 燃油压力调节器
18. fuel return pipe 燃油回油管
19. fuel rail 燃油管路
20. air cleaner 空气滤清器
21. air flow meter 空气流量计
22. throttle response 油门响应
23. routine maintenance 日常维护
24. fuel pressure 燃油压力
25. pressure regulator 压力调节器
26. electromagnetic coil 电磁线圈

Notes to Text

1. The function of the fuel supply system is to store and supply fuel to the cylinder chamber where it can be mixed with air, vaporized and burned to produce energy.
燃料供给系统的功能是储存燃油和给气缸室供应燃料,在那里其可以与空气混合、汽化、燃烧来产生能量。

2. Fuel injection system provides more exact air-fuel ratio control.
燃油喷射系统提供更精确的空燃比控制。

3. Most petrol injection systems are integrated with the ignition system into an engine management system, including three basic subsystems.

大多数汽油喷射系统与点火系统组成发动机管理系统，包括三个基本子系统。

4. The electronic control system of an engine is mainly composed of ECU, sensors and actuators.

发动机电子控制系统主要由电控单元、传感器和执行器组成。

5. As fuel is sprayed into the intake air stream, it mixes with the incoming air and vaporizes due to the low pressure in the intake manifold.

当燃料喷入进气流，由于进气歧管压力低，其发生汽化，并与进入的空气混合。

Exercises

1. Answer the following questions to the text.

(1) What is the function of the fuel supply system?

(2) What is the fuel supply system composed of?

(4) What do ECU and EFI mean?

(5) What are the advantages of EFI?

(6) What are the problems which routine maintenance of electronic-controlled gasoline injection system that should be paid attention to?

(7) What is the common trouble of electronic controlled gasoline injection system?

2. Translate the following phrases and expressions into Chinese.

(1) fuel supply system

(2) air-fuel ratio

(3) EFI

(4) intake manifold

(5) throttle response

(6) routine maintenance

3. Translate the following sentences into Chinese.

(1) A fuel pump draws the fuel from the tank through fuel lines and delivers it through a fuel filter to either a carburetor or fuel injector, then delivered to the cylinder chamber for combustion.

(2) Therefore, the electric fuel injection system has replaced the function of the carburetor in modern car engines.

(3) Most petrol injection systems are integrated with the ignition system into an engine management system, including three basic subsystems.

(4) Fuel is delivered from the tank to the injector by means of an electric fuel pump.

(5) The air induction system consists of air cleaner, air flow meter, throttle valve, air intake chamber, intake manifold runner, and intake valve.

Part Ⅲ Listening and Speaking

Automotive Testing A

A—Jenny B—Sue

A: Hey, Sue, that is a nice new car you have.
B: Thanks, I have been saving up for it for three years, ever since I heard your lecture on the testing of automobiles.
A: That's great, but I thought you were going to buy a hatchback, so you could transport a lot of things in the back.
B: I was, but the convertible is so much more attractive. Plus its normal trunk is fairly large.
A: If it makes you happy, you can't beat that.
B: That's the truth. Cars are created to make people happy and make work more convenient. And you know what? I just got a tune up. Now my car is faster than ever.
A: Is that all?
B: No, I also got a new horn. Now in case of emergencies, my horn is twice as loud, so it is twice as safe.
A: Safety first is the best policy. Look at that pickup truck, it is turning into oncoming traffic.
B: That is not safe.
A: Look, its windshield is also cracked, that is against the law.
B: I am glad I keep my car in good shape. I think we should get regular car test and oil changes whenever your car needs it for the sake of safety.
A: Some people treat their cars like their boyfriends or girlfriends. Most Americans even name their cars. Did you name yours?
B: Yes, I named mine Brad Pitt.
A: I should have guessed.

Automotive Testing B

A—Henry B—Mike

A: I heard that this car could rocket to 100 km per hour in just 3.8 seconds.
B: Yes, you are right. It is equipped with V10 engine.
A: I have no idea about engine things.

B: What's unique about the engine of this car is that the fuel is injected directly into the cylinder. For the driver, this leaves little lag time between pedal and acceleration. So it gives you gains in horsepower, gives you gains in torque. It also gives you better fuel economy, and it lowers emissions all at the same time.

A: Oh, that sounds great. But how can you know that engine is really so impressive?

B: Before being equipped on the car, the engine should go through a series of tests. After mounting the engine, the testing team attaches hoses to the intake and exhaust manifolds. Now the engine must prove it is worthy of the reputation. The team pushes it to perform at 8,700 rpm, normally the exclusive preserve of race engines.

A: Is that all?

B: No. For over an hour, the technicians check the engine's mechanical operation, fluid consumption, ignition system, electronics and sensors. Finally, they rev it to the max, to its limit of 8,700 rpm. At a blistering 950 degrees Celsius, the exhaust manifold turns red hot. Once the engine cools down, it moves to the assembly line.

Part IV Reading Material

Lean Combustion Technology and Cylinder Direct Injection Electronic Control Technology

Lean Combustion Technology

Thin burning, also called lean mixture combustion, is a way under the premise that the engine performance is guaranteed to improve fuel economy. Gasoline engine burning the best air and fuel ratio is 14.7 : 1, and thin combustion can reach above 20 : 1, this is not to reduce the fuel injection quantity, but in the case of the same fuel consumption, the engine intake more air to dilute mixture. Especially when the engine speed is very low, if intake air quantity increases, the mixture concentration is reduced, the combustion temperature is reduced, heat loss is reduced, that can use a longer time or mileage with the same amount of fuel. But thin combustion does not apply at high load and high speed when the power output is larger.

The biggest characteristic of thin combustion technology is high combustion efficiency, economy, environmental protection, at the same time it can also improve the engine power output.

The key technology of gasoline engine realizing lean combustion sums up has the following three main aspects:

Adopt compact chamber, through the inlet position improvements made from a strong air movement vortex in cylinder, improve air velocity. Put the spark plug in the center of combustion chamber, shortening the ignition distance. Improve the compression ratio to about 13 : 1, promoting the combustion speed.

If the mixing ratio of lean combustion technology reached 25 : 1 or above, it is not ignited according to conventional, so we must adopt from thick to thin stratified combustion mode. Around the spark plug form easy ignition rich mixture through the movement of air in the cylinder, mixing ratio has reached around 12 : 1, outer layer gradually thinning. Burning quickly spread to the outer after rich mixture ignited.

In order to improve the stability of combustion, reduce nitrogen oxides (NO_x), adopt the fuel injection timing and segmented injection technology. The injection is divided into two stages, the early admission injection, the fuel into the cylinder bottom first then evenly distributed inside the cylinder; intake late injection, thick mixture in the cylinder upper gathered was lit around the spark plug, realize the stratified combustion.

High energy ignition and wide gap spark plug are conducive to flame kernel, the distance of flame spread shortened, the combustion is rapid, lean burn limit is big. Some thin combustion engine adopts double spark plug or multi-electrode spark plugs device to achieve the above purpose.

The above three points only for overall gasoline engine thin combustion technology, specific to certain model will be overweight. Because technical measures of all sorts of gasoline engine thin combustion way are not identical, even the same engine under different conditions lean combustion way will not be exactly the same. Some focus on airflow movement in cylinder and the matching between the fuel distribution, the key in stratified combustion. Some focus on increasing ignition energy, fast increase flame propagation speed and shorten the flame propagation distance, the focus on high energy ignition.

Cylinder Direct Injection Electronic Control Technology

Gasoline Direct Injection (GDI) is to install the fuel nozzle in the cylinder, the fuel spray directly into the cylinder mixed with air inlet. Injection pressure is further improved, also makes the fuel atomization more careful, truly realized accurately proportional control injection and mixed with air inlet, and eliminates the defect of eject outside cylinder. At the same time, the position of the nozzle, spray shape, inlet air flow control, and shape of piston top special design, make oil and air fully and evenly mix in cylinder, so that the fuel combustion fully, the energy conversion efficiency is higher.

The main difference between injection in cylinder type gasoline engine and general gasoline engine is the location of the gasoline injection. Currently, in electronic controlled gasoline injection system used on general gasoline engine, gasoline is sprayed into the intake manifold or air intake pipe, mixed with air form the mixture and then through the inlet valve into the cylinder combustion chamber was lit and doing work. As the name suggests, injection in cylinder type gasoline engine is inject gas inside the cylinder, spray nozzle is installed in the combustion chamber, the gasoline is directly injected into the cylinder combustion chamber, the air is enters the combustion chamber through the inlet valve, mixed with gasoline form the mixture which was lit and doing work. This form is similar to direct injection diesel engine.

Injection in cylinder type gasoline engine has the advantage of low oil consumption, high power per liter. Mixing ratio reaches 40∶1 (mixing ratio of general petrol engine is 15∶1), which is what people call "lean burn". Half of piston top is spherical, and the other half is a wall. Air from the valve comes in, and forms a vortex motion under the compression of the piston. When the compression stroke is coming to an end, the spray nozzle at the top of the combustion chamber begins to spray oil, gas and air forms mixture under the effect of vortex motion. The rapidly rotating mixture is hierarchical, the more the mixture near the spark plug, the more it is thick, and the ignition works easily. Due to the injection in cylinder compression ratio reached 12, compared with the same volume general engine, power and torque is increased by 10%.

Stratified combustion technology is associated with the technology of cylinder direct injection (CDI). The real purpose of stratified combustion is to realize the lighting of lean mixture. Achieve stratified combustion must be based on GDI, for engine which injects outside cylinder is unable to realize the stratified combustion. The main purpose of designing the GDI is to realize the rarefied combustion. Lean combustion technology is to make the mixture more fully burn, and achieve the purpose of reducing fuel consumption and emission.

Unit 6 Supply and Combustion of Diesel Engine Fuel

Part I Illustrated English

Diagram of Diesel Engine Fuel System

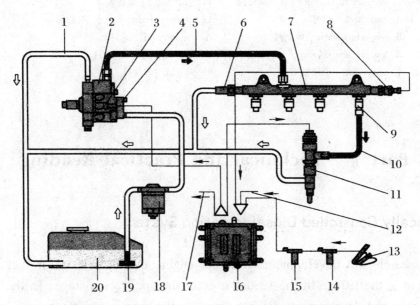

Fig. 6-1 The Basic Composition of Diesel Injection System

1. oil return tube   回油管
2. high-pressure pump   高压泵
3. solenoid valves   电磁阀
4. mechanical oil pump   机械输油泵
5./10. high-pressure oil tube   高压油管
6. pressure limiting valve   限压阀
7. high pressure memorizer   高压存储器
8. common rail pressure sensor   共轨压力传感器
9. flow limiter   流量限制器
11. electronic injector   电控喷油器
12. other sensors   其他传感器
13. accelerator pedal sensor   加速踏板传感器
14. camshaft position sensor   凸轮轴位置传感器
15. crankshaft position sensor   曲轴位置传感器
16. ECU   电控单元
17. other actuator   其他执行器
18. diesel filter   柴油滤清器
19. electric fuel pump   电动输油泵
20. fuel tank   油箱

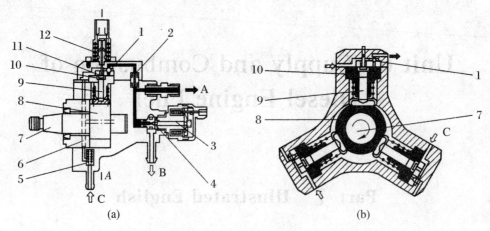

Fig. 6-2 High-pressure Pump

1. delivery valve 出油阀
2. seal components 密封件
3. pressure regulating valve 调压阀
4. ball check 球阀
5. non-return valve 单向阀
6. low-pressure oil-way 低压油路
7. drive shaft 驱动轴
8. eccentric cam 偏心凸轮
9. plunger pump element 柱塞泵油元件
10. plunger compartment 柱塞室
11. inlet valve 进油阀
12. electromagnetic valve 电磁阀
A. common rail 接共轨
B. oil return port 回油口
C. oil inlet 进油口

Part Ⅱ Technical and Practical Reading

Electronically Controlled Diesel Injection System

The research and development of diesel engine electronic control fuel injection system began in the 1970s. In the 1980s, it enter the application stage. In the 1990s, it has been the rapid development. It can improve the dynamic performance, economic performance and emission performance of the diesel engine produced great impact.

The traditional diesel injection system adopts mechanical means to regulate and control injection quantity and injection time. Due to the mechanical movement lag, the adjusting time is long, the accuracy is poor, injection rate, injection pressure and injection time is difficult to control, resulting in engine power and economy can not been given full play, and exhaust exceed the standard. The research shows that the general mechanical fuel injection system to the control precision of injection timing in about 2 degrees crank angle. The commencement of injection each change 1 degree crank angle, the rate of fuel consumption will increase by 2%, HC emissions by 6%, NO_x emissions by 6%.

Compared with the traditional mechanical diesel injection system, diesel engine electronic control fuel injection system has the following advantages:

The control accuracy of the injection timing is high, and reaction speed is fast. Control of the fuel injection quantity is accurate, flexible, fast, the fuel injection quantity can be adjusted optionally, and can achieve pre-injection and post-injection, and can change the fuel injection law. High injection pressure, is not affected by the engine speed, to optimize the combustion process. No parts wear, long-term good working stability. It has the advantages of simple structure, good reliability, strong adaptability, and can be used in the new and old engine.

The electronic diesel fuel injection system has experienced three generations.

The first generation of electronic control diesel injection system used position control system, which does not change the working principle and basic structure of the traditional fuel injection system. It just uses electronic components only, instead of the governor and timing advance unit. Its control frequency is low, its accuracy is not stable, its injection pressure is low, and its fuel injection rate is difficult to control, so it has been rarely used.

The second generation of the electronic control pump nozzle system of diesel engine is time control mode, it is characterized by using the electromagnetic valve directly controlled fuel injection start time and end time in the high-pressure oil way, to change the injection quantity and injection timing. It has direct control, the corresponding fast, high injection pressure, but unable to realize the flexible adjustment of injection pressure, and more difficult to achieve pre-injection or split injection.

The third generation of electronic control diesel injection system used electronic control common rail fuel injection system. It doesn't use plunger pump cylinder pulse supply principle of the injection system, but with a common rail pipe which has a larger volume set between the fuel pump and the fuel injector, store up the high pressure fuel pump output fuel and stable pressure, and then through the high pressure tubing conveyed to each injector, the electromagnetic valve on the injector controls injection start and termination. The injection system due to the injection pressure, injection timing, injection quantity and injection rate adjustable, superior performance, is widely used in modern diesel cars.

The following are highlights.

The high pressure common rail fuel injection system is mainly composed of the fuel supply system and the electronic control system.

The Fuel Supply System

The fuel supply system consists of two parts which are low pressure oil and high pressure oil.

Low-pressure oil way consists of tank, electric fuel pump, mechanical pump and diesel filter, etc. Its purpose is to produce low pressure diesel and sends to the high-pressure pump. Its structure and working principle is similar to low-pressure oil way in the traditional supply system of the diesel engine.

High-pressure oil way is composed of high-pressure oil pump, high-pressure oil pipe, high pressure memory and injector, etc. Its basic function is to generate high-pressure diesel.

High-pressure Pump

Its role is to produce high-pressure oil. It adopts three plunger pump oil elements which are radially arranged and staggered 120°. They are driven by the eccentric cam. The oil output is large, and the load is uniform.

Pressure Regulating Valve

It is installed in the high-pressure pump side or common rail pipe, is according to the condition of the engine load adjust and maintain pressure of the common rail.

High-pressure Accumulator (Common Rail)

It is the role of high pressure oil storage, keep the pressure stable. The common rail pressure sensor, a pressure limiting valve and a flow restrictor are installed on the common rail pipe. The common rail pressure sensor through the fixed screw fastening in the common rail pipe, the internal pressure sensing diaphragm feels the common rail pressure. Through the analysis of the circuit, the pressure signal is converted to the electrical signal pass to the ECU to control. The pressure limiting valve is to limit the pressure in the common rail pipe. When the pressure exceeds the spring force, open valve to relief the pressure, high pressure oil flow through holes and oil return hole flow back to the tank. Flow limiter can prevent the injector from appearing continuous injection.

Electronic controlled injector

It is the core component of common rail fuel injection system, its role is to accurately control the injection time, injection quantity and injection law. The electronic controlled injector mainly consists of the injector nozzle matching parts and solenoid valves.

Electronic Control System

The electronic control system is composed of sensors, electronic control unit (ECU) and the executive mechanism.

The injection quantity, injection time and injection law of high pressure common rail diesel injector, in addition depends on engine speed, load, but also relate to many factors, such as the inlet flow, inlet temperature, coolant temperature, oil temperature, loading pressure, voltage, camshaft position, exhaust emission, etc., so we must use the corresponding sensor to collect relevant data. The sensor structure and working principle is almost the same as the sensor of electronically controlled gasoline injection system.

Data collected by all kinds of sensors are sent to ECU, and compared with and analyzed the large quantities of data which storing on the inside, including the optimal fuel injection quantity, the injection time and injection rate which got after the test. Calculate the optimal parameters of the current state, the speed up to 20 million times per second.

The optimum parameters calculated by ECU, then go back through the actuator (solenoid valve) control electronic injector, high pressure oil pump and other work institutions, so that the fuel injector according to the optimal amount of fuel injection, injection time and injection law for injection.

New Words

1. combustion [kəmˈbʌstʃən] n. 燃烧，烧毁；氧化；骚动
2. injection [ɪnˈdʒɛkʃən] n. 注射；注射剂
3. valve [vælv] n. 阀；真空管；(管乐器的)活栓
4. memorizer [ˈmɛməraɪzər] n. 存储器
5. sensor [ˈsɛnsɚ, -ˌsɔr] n. 传感器，灵敏元件
6. accelerator [ækˈsɛləˌretɚ] n. 加速器；催速剂
7. camshaft [ˈkæmʃæft] n. 凸轮轴
8. crankshaft [ˈkræŋkʃæft] n. 机轴；曲轴
9. actuator [ˈæktʃʊˌeɪtə] n. 执行机构；促动器
10. cam [kæm] n. 凸轮
11. plunger [ˈplʌndʒɚ] n. 手压皮碗泵；撞针杆；活塞
12. lag [læg] v. 走得极慢，落后；落后于
13. exhaust [ɪɡˈzɔst] v. 用尽，耗尽；使筋疲力尽；排出
14. emissions [ɪˈmɪʃənz] n. 排放物 (emission 的名词复数形式)
15. wear [wer] v. 磨损；耗损
16. reliability [rɪˌlaɪəˈbɪlətɪ] n. 可靠，可信赖
17. adaptability [əˌdæptəˈbɪlətɪ] v. 适应性；合用性
18. overall [ˌoʊvərˈɔl] adj. 全部的；全体的
19. generation [ˌdʒɛnəˈreʃən] n. 一代人；一代(约30年)，时代
20. nozzle [ˈnɑzl] n. 管嘴，喷嘴
21. electromagnetic [ɪˌlɛktroʊmæɡˈnɛtɪk] adj. 电磁的
22. highlights [ˈhaɪlaɪts] n. 亮点；重点
23. solenoid [ˈsoʊlənɔɪd] n. 螺线管；线包
24. coolant [ˈkulənt] n. 冷冻剂，冷却液，散热剂
25. optimal [ˈɑptɪməl] n. 最佳的，最优的；最理想的
26. parameters [pəˈræmɪtəz] n. 参量；参项；决定因素

Phrases and Expressions

1. fuel injection system   燃油喷射系统
2. dynamic performance   动力性能
3. economic performance   经济性能
4. emission performance   排放性能
5. injection rate   喷油速率
6. compared with   与……相比
7. injection timing   喷油定时
8. pre-injection   预喷射
9. post-injection   后喷射
10. overall composition   总体组成

11. working principle　工作原理
12. common rail　共轨
13. fuel supply system　燃油供给系统
14. low-pressure oil way　低压油路
15. high-pressure oil way　高压油路
16. pressure regulating valve　调压阀
17. electronic control system　电子控制系统

Notes to Text

1. The traditional diesel injection system adopts mechanical means to regulate and control injection quantity and injection time.

传统的柴油机喷射系统采用机械方式进行喷油量和喷油时间的调节与控制。

2. Compared with the traditional mechanical diesel injection system, diesel engine electronic control fuel injection system has the following advantages.

与传统的机械柴油喷射系统相比，电控柴油喷射系统具有如下优点。

3. Control of the fuel injection quantity is accurate, flexible, fast, the fuel injection quantity can be adjusted optionally, and can achieve pre-injection and post-injection, change the fuel injection law.

对喷油量的控制精确、灵活、快速，喷油量可随意调节，还可实现预喷射和后喷射，改变喷油规律。

4. The injection system due to the injection pressure, injection timing, injection quantity and injection rate adjustable, superior performance, is widely used in modern diesel cars.

这种喷射系统因其喷油压力、喷油时间、喷油量及喷油规律可调节，且性能优越而被现代电控柴油汽车广泛采用。

5. The high pressure common rail fuel injection system is mainly composed of the fuel supply system and the electronic control system.

高压共轨电控柴油喷射系统主要由燃油供给系统和电子控制系统两大部分组成。

Exercises

1. Answer the following questions to the text.
   (1) What are the disadvantages of the traditional diesel injection system?
   (2) What are the advantages of the diesel engine electronic control fuel injection system?
   (3) Which generations of the electronic diesel fuel injection system has experienced?
   (4) What is the overall composition of electronic diesel fuel injection system?
   (5) What is the working principle of electronic diesel fuel injection system?

2. Translate the following phrases and expressions into Chinese.
   (1) oil return tube
   (2) high-pressure pump
   (3) pressure limiting valve

(4) camshaft position sensor

(5) low-pressure oil-way

(6) non-return valve

3. Translate the following sentences into Chinese.

(1) Due to the mechanical movement lag, the adjusting time is long, the accuracy is poor, injection rate, injection pressure and injection time is difficult to control, resulting in engine power and economy can not been given full play.

(2) The control accuracy of the injection timing is high, and reaction speed is fast.

(3) No parts wear, long-term good working stability.

(4) Its control frequency is low, its accuracy is not stable, its injection pressure is low, and its fuel injection rate is difficult to control, so it has been rarely used.

(5) The injection system due to the injection pressure, injection timing, injection quantity and injection rate adjustable, superior performance, is widely used in modern diesel cars.

(6) The electronic control system is composed of sensors, electronic control unit (ECU) and the executive mechanism.

Part Ⅲ   Listening and Speaking

Manufacturing Process A

A—Journalist B—Dr. Thomas

A: Hello, Dr. Thomas, I'm the journalist from *China Daily*. Can I ask you some questions about the production process of Audi R8?

B: Of course.

A: As the head of production process, R8, can you give us a brief introduction about the production of R8?

B: Well. It takes one mega factory and many suppliers to build the R8. Audi's factory in Neckarsulm, Germany builds the R8 body, chassis and interior. More than 4,500 people who work here also build the A6 and the A8 sedans. But just 120 of the factory's best workers are qualified to work on the prestigious R8 assembly line. On an average work day, the factory turns out only 20 R8s. Each car is manufactured in the true sense of the word. It is built largely by hand.

A: It sounds that the production of R8 is a process of producing a piece of artwork. So how many phases are involved in this process?

B: R8 production takes place in three main halls within dedicated buildings at the factory. The process starts in the body shop where workers laser-weld aluminum parts and panels into bodies, then the paint shop where R8s get their sleek finished. Next, the assembly hall where workers finally transform the painted body into a road-going powerhouse.

A: It's really impressive. Can I have a visit to your production factory?

B: Certainly, this way, please.

Manufacturing Process B

A—Mr. Johnson   B—Mr. Kraft

A: How do you do, Mr. Kraft? I've been expecting you.

B: It's good of you to show me around. Your plant is much smaller than I expected.

A: Our small size makes us very flexible. As you know, the automobile industry is much influenced by trends and fashion. Style changes from year to year. Because of the small size, we can respond to changes quickly.

B: Yes, your company has a good reputation in the field. Well, shall we get started on our tour?

A: I suggest we start at the beginning of our production line.

B: Fine. How long have you been in automobile industry?

A: I began in 1992.

B: Does your factory carry out the entire process of manufacturing?

A: Almost. A few necessary items like lights, windows, seats, and windshield wipers are made elsewhere. Then they are checked for quality at our factory and added to the automobiles.

B: Nowadays there is a lot of competition in the automobile industry, so how does your factory stand out from all the others?

A: First we find it important for us to be rigid in checking the quality of products. Besides, every year we spend a lot of money on research and development. And by introducing advanced technologies, the production method has been improved a lot.

B: Well, thank you for showing me around. Well, your factory impressed me a lot, but I'd like to study them a bit further.

A: Well, I'll be waiting for you to discuss further.

B: I'm looking forward to cooperating with your factory.

A: I'm sure that our products will meet the standards you expect.

Part Ⅳ   Reading Material

Combustion of Diesel Engine

The Formation of Mixed Gas of Diesel Engine

  The diesel engine uses diesel as the fuel, which can only be sprayed directly into the cylinder before TDC on the compression stroke and ignited by compression because of its evaporation and liquidity are worse than gasoline and the self-ignition point is lower than that of gasoline.

Because the mixture of the diesel engine formed in a very short period of time, accounted for only 15 degrees to 35 degrees crankshaft angle (3,000 r/min meter according to engine speed, accounted for only $8.3 \times 10^4 \sim 1.9 \times 10^{-3}$ s), the air-fuel mixture's formation is very difficult, and the combustion is in the same time with injection, the mixture in cylinder concentration is rather inhomogeneous, which is extremely easy to cause incomplete combustion, black smoke exhaust, power and economy performance decrease and other adverse consequences.

Therefore, in addition to the high-pressure fuel injection described before, the modern diesel engine also need to organize the air in the cylinder to form the high-speed flow, and at the same time, design various combustion chamber to promote the combustible mixture formation and rapid combustion.

It can be divided into two basic modes for mixed space atomization and mixing and oil film evaporation according to the forming characteristics of the diesel engine mixed gas. The space atomization mixture sprays diesel into the combustion chamber space with high-pressure and forms fog mixed with air. In order to make uniform mixing, the sprayed fuel should match the combustion chamber shape, and make full use of the air motion in the combustion chamber. Oil film evaporation injects most of the diesel fuel into the combustion chamber wall, forms a layer of oil film, which will evaporate when being heated, the fuel vapor and air can form combustible mixed gas uniformly under strongly rotating airflow in the combustion chamber. In the actual diesel injection, it is difficult to ensure a complete fuel spray into the combustion chamber space or the wall surface of the combustion chamber, so there are two kinds of mixed mode, just how many different priorities.

In order to promote the fuel and air mixture, the proper organization of the air vortex is needed. There are three common species: intake swirl, extrusion, and eddy turbulence combustion.

Intake swirl refers to the air entering the cylinder forms of air rotating in a high-speed around cylinder center on the intake stroke. It continues to combustion expansion process.

Generally, method of generating intake swirl is to design the inlet into a spiral inlet or tangential inlet. The tangential air inlet has a strong contraction before the valve seat, directing the flow of air into the cylinder with unilateral tangential direction, and causing swirl. The spiral intake port is piped into a spiral shape in the valve at the top of valve seat, this makes the flow form a certain intensity of rotation in the helical port, resulting in a strong swirl and eddy current speed can reach the speed of the crankshaft 6~10 times.

Extrusion refers to the air movement formed in the compression process. When the piston is close to compression TDC, gas in the annular space part of upper piston top is squeezed into the pit in the top of the piston, formed the motion of the gas. When the piston goes down, air in the pit in the top of the piston flows into the annular space outside, known as inverse extrusion flow. The production of extrusion has a great relationship with the design of piston's top vortex pits, there are various of diesel engine piston's top vortex pits which to promote mixing and combustion of fuel and air.

Eddy turbulence combustion refers to the impact of unburned gas mixture with the use of diesel combustion energy, causing the mixture turbulence or vortex. The aim is to promote fuel and air mixing and combustion further. The degree of combustion and diesel turbulent vortex machine is closely related to the shape of the combustion chamber.

The Diesel Engine Combustion Chamber

The combustion chamber is the site of diesel engine combustion. It has an important effect on the combustion, and the structure is various. It can be divided into two categories which are the direct injection combustion chamber and the separated combustion chamber basically.

The Direct Injection Combustion Chamber

The mechanism characteristics of direct injection combustion chamber is it has only one combustion chamber, which located between the top surface of the piston and the cylinder cover bottom plane, fuel injected directly into the combustion chamber and mixed with air for combustion. The piston top design of the direct injection combustion chamber is highly original, different gas vortex pits, different movement, and different mixture formation, resulting in differences in engine performance.

The Separated Combustion Chamber

The structure characteristics of separated combustion chamber is that it is separated into the main combustion chamber and the auxiliary combustion chamber which are interlinked with one or two channels. The auxiliary combustion chamber is in the cylinder head, the volume is 50% ~ 80% of total compressed volume, the main combustion chamber is in the bottom of the cylinder head plane and the piston top surface. The fuel will inject into the auxiliary combustion chamber in the cylinder head to have the pre-combustion, and then has a further combustion through the channel across the main combustion chamber on the piston crown.

Unit 7　Gasoline Engine Ignition System

Part Ⅰ　Illustrated English

Diagram of Engine Ignition System with and without Distributor

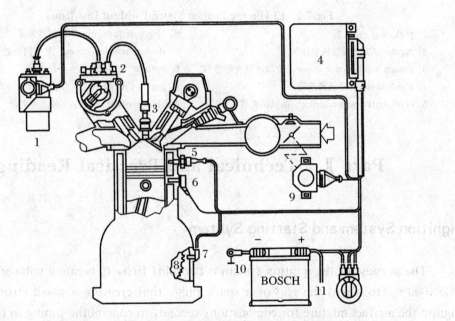

Fig. 7-1　EI (Engine Ignition System) with Distributor

1. ignition coil with igniter　带点火器的点火线圈
2. ignition distributor　分电器
3. spark plug　火花塞
4. engine ECU　发动机电控单元
5. coolant temperature sensor　冷却液温度传感器
6. knock sensor　爆震传感器
7. crankshaft position sensor　曲轴位置传感器
8. ring gear for sensor　传感器齿圈
9. throttle position sensor　节气门位置传感器
10. battery　蓄电池
11. ignition switch　点火开关

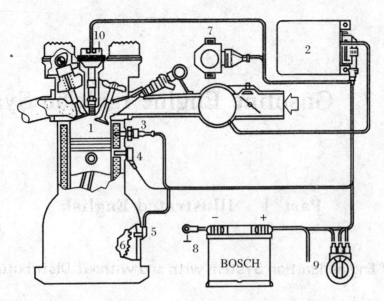

Fig. 7-2 EI (Engine Ignition System) without Distributor

1. park plug   火花塞
2. engine ECU   发动机电控单元
3. coolant temperature sensor   冷却液温度传感器
4. knock sensor   爆震传感器
5. crankshaft position sensor   曲轴位置传感器
6. ring gear for sensor   传感器齿圈
7. throttle position sensor   节气门位置传感器
8. battery   蓄电池
9. ignition switch   点火开关
10. independent ignition   独立点火器

Part Ⅱ Technical and Practical Reading

Ignition System and Starting System

The purpose of the ignition system is twofold: first, to create a voltage high enough (20,000+) to across the gap of a spark plug, thus creating a spark strong enough to ignite the air-fuel mixture for combustion; second, to control the timing so that the spark occurs at the right time and at the right cylinder.

The basic principle of the electrical spark ignition system has not changed for over 75 years. What has changed is the method by which the spark is created. The automobile has evolved from a mechanical system (distributor) to a solid state electronic system. Both systems control a low voltage primary circuit through an ignition coil which will include a high voltage in the secondary circuit which is then directed to the right spark plug at the right time.

Primary Circuit

The primary circuit consists of an ignition switch, a ballast resistor, some types of off/on switches, (a set of breaker points in the older cars), which is usually inside a distributor, an ignition coil and the connecting wires. The purpose of the primary circuit is to allow low voltage from the battery, to pass through the ignition coil where the voltage is stepped up from 12 volts to as much as 40,000 volts.

Ignition Coil

The ignition coil contains both the primary and the secondary winding circuits. The coil primary winding contains 100 to 150 turns of heavy copper wire. The turns of this wire must be insulated from each other or they would short out and not create the primary magnetic field that is required. The primary circuit wire goes into the coil through the positive terminal and exits through the negative terminal. The coil secondary winding circuit contains 15,000 to 30,000 turns of fine copper wire, which also must be insulated from each other. To withstand the heat of the current flow, the coil is filled with oil for cooling. The ignition coil is the heart of the ignition system. As current flows through the coil, a strong magnetic field is built up. When the current is shut off, the collapse of this magnetic field induces a high voltage which is released through the large center terminal through the distributor to the spark plugs.

Secondary Circuit

The secondary circuit consists of the secondary windings of the ignition coil, which produces through a high tension wire to the distributor cap where a rotor distributes the spark through the distributor cap, to the right spark plug at the right time.

Breaker Points

Breaker points have not been used since the mid-1970s, but many older cars still have them. Because of the simplicity of breaker points, it is a good starting point in understanding the switching mechanism that controls the current flow through the coil. The points are made up of a fixed contact point and a movable contact point. The movable point is spring loaded and rides on a 4-, 6-, or 8-lobe cam (depending on the number of cylinders). The points are located inside a distributor. As the engine rotates, the camshaft turns the distributor, which then opens and closes the breaker points as many as 15,000 to 25,000 times a minute. When the points are closed, current is allowed to flow through the ignition coil, thereby building a magnetic field around the windings. When the points are opened, they interrupt that current flow, thereby collapsing the magnetic field and releasing a high voltage surge. This high voltage enters the top of the distributor, where an ignition rotor distributes that voltage through a cap to the right spark plug at the right time. The distributor also contains a condenser that prevents arcing by absorbing excess current when the points open. The difficulty with the breaker points system is that the part that rubs against the cm wears. This wear causes a constant need for adjustment and eventual replacement. In the mid-1970s, this problem was corrected through the use of solid state electronics and transistors as switching devices.

The starting system, the heart of the electrical system in your car, begins with the battery. The key is inserted into the ignition switch and then turned to the start position. As small amount of current then passes through the neutral safety switch to a starter relay or a starter solenoid which allow high current to flow through the battery cables to the starter motor. The starter motor then cranks the engine so that the piston, moving downward, can create a suction that will draw a fuel-air mixture into the cylinder, where a spark created by the igniting system will ignite this mixture. If the compression in the engine is high enough and all these happen at the right time, the engine will start.

Battery

The automotive battery, also known as a lead-acid storage battery, is an electrochemical device that produces voltage and delivers current. In an automotive battery, we can reverse the electrochemical action, thereby recharging the battery, which will then give us many years of services. The purpose of the battery is to supply additional current when the demand is higher than the alternator can supply and to act as an electrical reservoir.

Ignition Switch

The ignition switch allows the driver to distribute electrical current to where it is needed. There are generally five key switch positions that are used:

Lock-All circuits are open (no current supplied) and the steering wheel is in the lack position. In some cars, the transmission lever cannot be moved in this position. If the steering wheel is applying pressure to the locking mechanism, the key might be hard to turn. If you do experience this type of condition, try moving the steering wheel to remove the pressure as you turn the key.

Off-All circuits are open, but the steering wheel can be burned and the key cannot be extracted.

Run-All circuits, except the starter circuit, are closed (current is allowed to pass through). Current is supplied to all but the starter circuit. Start-Power is supplied to the ignition circuit and the starter motor only. That is why the radio stops playing in the start position. This position of the ignition switch is spring loader so that the starter is not engaged while the engine is running. This position is used momentarily, just to activate the starter. Accessory-Power is supplied to all but the ignition and starter circuit. This allows you to play the radio, work the power windows, etc., while the engine is not running. Most ignition switches are mounted on the steering column. Some switches are actually two separate parts. The lock into which you insert the key also contains the mechanism to lock the steering wheel and shifter. The switch contains the actual electrical circuits. It is usually mounted on the top of the steering column just behind the dash and is connected to the lock by a linkage or a rod.

Neutral Safety Switch

This switch opens (denies current to) the starter circuit when the transmission is in any gear but neutral of park on automatic transmissions. This switch is normally connected to the transmission linkage or directly on the transmission. Most cars utilize the same switch to apply current to the back up lights when the transmission is put in reverse. Standard transmission cars will connect this switch to the clutch pedal so that the starter will not engage unless the clutch pedal is pressed. If you find that you have to move the shifter away from park or neutral to get the car to start, if usually means that this switch needs adjustment. If your car has an automatic parking brake release, the neutral safety switch will also control that function.

Starter Relay

A relay is a device that allows a small amount of electrical current to control a large amount of current. An automobile starter uses a large amount of current (250 + amps) to start an engine. If we were to allow that much current to go through the ignition switch, we would not only need a very large switch, but all the wires would have to be the size of battery cables (not very practical). A starter relay is installed in series between the battery and the starter. Some cars use a starter solenoid to accomplish the same purpose of allowing a small amount of current from the ignition switch to control a high current flow from the battery to the starter. The starter solenoid in some cases also mechanically engages the starter gear with the engine.

Battery Cables

Battery cables are large diameter, multi-stand wires which carry the high current (250 + amps) necessary to operate the starter motor. Some have a smaller wire soldered to the terminal which is used to either operate a smaller device or provide an additional ground. When the smaller cable burns, this indicates a high resistance in the heavy cable. Care must be taken to keep the battery cable ends (terminals) clean and tight. Battery cables can be replaced with ones that are slightly larger but never smaller.

Starter Motor

The starter motor is a powerful electric motor, with a small gear attached to the end. When activated, the gear is meshed with a larger gear ring, which is attached to the engine. The starter motor then spins the engine over so that the piston can draw in fuel-air mixture, which is then ignited to start the engine. When the engine starts to spin faster than the starter, a device called an overrunning clutch (bendix drive) automatically disengages the starter gear from the engine gear.

New Words

1. twofold ['tu:fould] adj. 双重的
2. gap [gæp] n. 间隙,缝隙
3. right [raɪt] adj. 合适的,恰当的
4. distributor [dɪ'strɪbjətə] n. 分电器
5. breaker ['brekə] n. 断电器
6. volt [voult] n. 伏特
7. winding ['waɪndɪŋ] n. 绕组,线圈
8. circuit ['sɜːrkɪt] n. 电路
9. coil [kɔɪl] n. 线圈
10. copper ['kɑːpə(r)] n. 铜
11. insulate ['ɪnsəleɪt] v. 使绝缘,使隔离
12. positive ['pɑːzətɪv] adj. 正的,阳性的
13. negative ['nɛɡətɪv] adj. 负的,阴性的
14. terminal ['tɜːrmɪnl] n. 末端,终端,终点站
15. iron ['aɪərn] n. 铁
16. withstand [wɪθ'stænd, wɪð-] v. 承受;抵制
17. collapse [kə'læps] n. 倒塌,崩溃,衰竭
18. tower ['tauə] n. 支架,支柱
19. current ['kɜːrənt] n. 电流
20. simplicity [sɪm'plɪsɪti] n. 简单
21. resistor [rɪ'zɪstə] v. [电]电阻器
22. condenser [kən'dɛnsə] n. 电容器
23. transistor [træn'zɪstə] n. 晶体管
24. rub [rʌb] v. 擦,摩擦
25. starter ['stɑːrtə(r)] n. 起动机
26. relay ['riːleɪ] n. 继电器
27. solenoid ['soulənɔɪd] n. [电]螺线管
28. electrochemical [ɪˌlektrou'kemɪkəl] adj. 电气化学的
29. alternator ['ɔːltərneɪtə(r)] n. 交流发电机
30. extract [ɪk'strækt] v. 抽取
31. engage [ɪn'ɡedʒ] v. 接合,连接
32. accessory [æk'sɛsəri] n. 附件
33. neutral ['nuːtrəl] n. (汽车)空挡
34. pedal ['pɛdl] n. 踏板
35. shifter ['ʃɪftər] n. 变速杆
36. strand [strænd] n. 线,绳
37. disengage [ˌdɪsɛn'ɡedʒ] v. 使解脱,分离

Phrases and Expressions

1. ignition system 点火系统
2. starting system 起动系统
3. spark plug 火花塞
4. ignition coil 点火线圈
5. ignition switch 点火开关
6. ballast resistor 平衡电阻器
7. breaker point 断电器触点
8. secondary winding 次级线圈
9. magnetic field 磁场
10. positive terminal 正极
11. negative terminal 负极
12. soft iron 软铁
13. center tower 中心电极
14. distributor cap 分电器盖
15. high tension wire 高压线,高压电路
16. high voltage surge 高压浪涌
17. transmission lever 变速器杆
18. power window 电动车窗
19. steering column 转向柱
20. gear ring 齿圈

21. bendix drive 邦迪克斯起动机惯性啮合传动机构
22. overrunning clutch 单向离合器

Notes to Text

1. The purpose of the primary circuit is to allow low voltage from the battery, to pass through the ignition coil where the voltage is stepped up from 12 volts to as much as 40,000 volts.

初级电路的目的是把来自蓄电池的低压,通过点火线圈的传递,逐步将电压从12伏增加到40,000伏。

2. The turns of this wire must be insulated from each other or they would short out and not create the primary magnetic field that is required.

这些成匝的粗铜线必须彼此绝缘,否则它们将发生短路,不能产生所要求的初级磁场。

3. A small amount of current then passes through the neutral safety switch to a starter relay or a starter solenoid which allows high current to flow through the battery cables to the starter motor.

低值电流通过空挡安全开关传递到起动机继电器或起动机电磁线圈处,在那里产生高值电流通过蓄电池电缆流至起动机电机处。

4. Some cars use a starter solenoid to accomplish the same purpose of allowing a small amount of current from the ignition switch to control a high current flow from the battery to the starter.

有一些车采用的是起动机电磁线圈,它同样可以达到让来自于点火开关的低值电流去控制从蓄电池到起动机之间流动的高值电流的目的。

Exercises

1. **Answer the following questions to the text.**

   (1) What is the basic principle of the igniting system?
   (2) Why is the ignition coil the heart of the ignition system?
   (3) What does the starting system consist of?
   (4) Explain five key switch positions that are used generally, please.
   (5) What is the purpose of the igniting system?

2. **Translate the following phrases and expressions into Chinese.**

   (1) ballast resistor
   (2) magnetic field
   (3) breaker point
   (4) overrunning clutch
   (5) positive terminal
   (6) power window

3. Translate the following sentences into Chinese.

(1) The purpose of the primary circuit is to allow low voltage from the battery, to pass through the ignition coil where the voltage is stepped up from 12 bolts to as much as 40,000 volts.

(2) When the current is shut off, the collapse of this magnetic field induces a high voltage which is released through the large center terminal through the distributor to the spark plug.

(3) The purpose of the battery is to supply current to the starter motor, to provide current to the ignition system while cranking, to supply additional current when the demand is higher than the alternator can supply and to act as an electrical reservoir.

(4) Standard transmission cars will connect this switch to the clutch pedal so that the starter will not engage unless the clutch pedal is depressed.

(5) If we were to allow that much current to go through the ignition switch, we would not only need a very large switch, but all the wires would have to be the size of battery cables (not very practical).

Part Ⅲ Listening and Speaking

Automotive Outsourcing A

A—Paul   B—Richard

A: Body is very important for automotive production. Nowadays, many models use aluminum to construct their bodies.

B: Yes, you are right. The use of aluminum slashes the frame weight down to less than half the weight of a steel frame. A lighter body means better faster speed. Aluminum technology is one of the most significant advances in automotive construction in recent history. It really provides the ability to lightweight vehicles and provides excellent strength.

A: How do those aluminum body panels come out?

B: The manufacturing process begins when pure aluminum ingots, called pigs, arrive from a smelter. Then a 54-ton crane loads the pigs into a massive melting furnace. The ingots take four to six hours to melt, even in the heat that reaches 730 Celsius. Other metals like magnesium and silicon go into the mix. The fiery liquid becomes an alloy specially reserved for automotive panels. A process called fluxing brings impurities in the aluminum to the surface. From then, a worker skims them off. Then the liquefied aluminum alloy pours into moulds. Just four minutes later, a massive ingot emerges.

A: How large are those ingot?
B: The thickness out of casting pit is 24 inches by 54 inches wide by 207 inches long.
A: Is that all?
B: Not for sure. We just completed casting this ingot. That thickness will be rolled down eventually to approximately 1 cm or less.
A: So, how can we achieve that?
B: The aluminum ingots now head to a hot rolling line on a 54-ton crane. By repeatedly passing heated aluminum ingots back and forth, the rollers will flatten the ingots into thin sheets. There, almost six million kilograms of pressure make dough out of metal. The furnace heats the ingot to 450 degrees Celsius. This temperature allows the ingot to be rolled to the thickness needed for car panels. A lubricant prevents the ingot from sticking to the rollers. With each pass through the hot rollers, the ingot becomes thinner and longer. After 18 to 20 passes, a half-metre thick ingot can flatten to a sheet just 1 cm thick. It stretches to 15 times its original length.
A: Wow, it is really only 1 cm thick? It's amazing.
B: That's right. At this stage, it's ready for spooling. From the conveyor, the stretched-out ingot rolls on itself into a coil. It looks like a mega roll of aluminum foil. This roll weighs about 9,000 kg. Now Alcoa ships the coil to another supplier for stamping and forming. This is where a car panel gets its shape.
A: The production of a car is really a complicated and scientific process.

Automotive Outsourcing B

A—Manager B—Guest

A: Our factory has established a manufacturing line which consists of injection workshop, seats workshop, stamp workshop, frame workshop, and assembly workshop. I'll show you around and explain the operation as we go along.
B: That'll be most helpful.
A: Put on the helmet, please.
B: Do we need to put on the jackets too?
A: Yes, you'd better protect your clothes. Now please watch your step.
B: Thank you. Is the production line fully automated?
A: Yes, almost automated. The whole assembly line owns higher mechanization degree and advanced production technology. The most parts of the manufacturing process are strictly controlled by computer which ensures every link in the production chain efficiently and precisely.
B: Well, it's very impressive. I found that your factory obtains good technology in process.
A: Yes, we have the best technology from the first-rate international company as our backup supporting.

B: I see. How do you control the quality?

A: All products have to go through five checks in the whole manufacturing process.

B: Well, the whole process is highly controlled.

A: Exactly. This is our stamp workshop. Please go this way. As we know, stamping plays an important role in the production process. It is one of the most fundamental methods for metal processing. A great number of automotive parts are molded by stamping. What you are watching now is the machine presses car bodies out of sheets of steel.

B: That's wonderful. Is that where the finished products come off?

A: Yes. Let me show you the other workshops of our factory. Please go this way.

Part IV Reading Material

Automotive Electrical System

The electrical system of the automobile was, at first limited to the ignition equipment. However, electric lights and horns began to replace the kerosene and acetylene lights and the bulb horns with the advent of the electric starter on a 1912 model. Electrification was rapid and complete, and by 1930, six-volt systems were standard everywhere. The electrical system consists of a storage battery, generator, starting (cranking) motor, lighting system, ignition system, and various accessories and controls.

It was difficult to meet high ignition voltage requirements with the increased engine speeds and higher cylinder pressure of the post-World War II cars. The larger engines required higher cranking torque. Additional electrically operated features, such as radios, window regulators, and multispeed windshield wipers, also added to system requirements. 12-volt systems generally replaced the 6-volt systems in 1956 production to meet these needs.

The ignition system consists of the spark plugs, coil, distributor, and battery, and provides the spark to ignite the air-fuel mixture in the cylinder of the engine. In order to jump the gap between the electrodes of the spark plugs, the 12-volt potential of the electrical system must be stepped up to about 20,000 volts. This happens with the aid of a circuit that starts with the battery, one side of which is grounded on the chassis and leads through the ignition switch to the primary winding of the ignition coil and back to the ground through an interrupter switch. A high-voltage induced across the secondary of the coil by interrupting the primary circuit. The high-voltage secondary terminal of the coil leads to a distributor that acts as a rotary switch, alternately connecting the coil to each of the wires leading to the spark plugs.

It was in the 1970s that solid-state or transistorized ignition systems were introduced. Increased durability by eliminating the frictional contacts between breaker points and distributor cams was provided by these distributor systems. A revolving magnetic pulse generator in which alternating-current pulses trigger the high voltage needed for ignition by means of an amplifier electronic circuit replaced the breaker points. Changes in engine ignition timing are made by vacuum or electronic control unit (microprocessor) connections to the distributor.

The generator is the basic source of energy for the various electrical devices of the automobile. An alternator that is belt-driven from the engine crankshaft is also used at times. The design is usually an alternating-current type with built-in rectifiers and a voltage regulator to match the generator output to the electric load and also to the charging requirements of the battery, regardless of engine speed.

To store excess output of the generator, a lead-acid battery is used which serves as a reservoir. Energy for the starting motor is thus made available along with power for operating other electric devices when the engine is not running or when the generator speed is not sufficiently high to cater the load.

The starting motor then drives a small spur gear, which is so arranged that it automatically moves into mesh with gear teeth on the rim of the flywheel as the starting-motor armature begins to turn. As soon as the engine starts, the gear is disengaged, to prevent the starting motor from getting damaged due to over-speeding. The starting motor is designed for high current consumption and delivers considerable power for its size for a limited time.

Night driving has long been dangerous due to the glare of headlights that blind drivers approaching from the opposite direction. Therefore, headlights that satisfactorily illuminate the highway ahead of the automobile for night driving without temporarily blinding approaching drivers have long been sought. To correct this problem, resistance-type dimming circuits, which decreased the brightness of the headlights when meeting another car, were first introduced. This gave way to mechanical tilting reflectors and later to double-filament bulbs with a high and a low beam, called sealed beam units.

There was only one filament at the focal point of the reflector in the double-filament headlight unit of necessity. Greater illumination required for high-speed driving with the high beam, consequently, the lower beam filament was placed off center, with a resulting decrease in lighting effectiveness. From the 1950s, manufactures equipped their models with four headlights to improve illumination.

In some cars, dimming is automatically achieved. This happens by means of a photocell-controlled switch in the lamp circuit that is triggered by the lights of an oncoming car. Larger double-filament lamps and halogen-filled lamp bulbs with improved photometric permitted a return to two-headlight systems on some cars. At many places, the law limits the total intensity of forward lighting systems to 75,000 candlepower (800,000 lux).

In most new automobiles, lowering front hood heights for improved aerodynamic drag and driver visibility reduces the vertical height available for headlights. Due to this, lower-profile rectangular sealed-beam units and higher-intensity bulbs, in conjunction with partial parabolic reflectors with reduced vertical axis, were adopted in the 1970s. In some cases, models featured full-size concealed headlights that were not visible until turned on. An electric motor linkage was used to rotate the lamp housing or a housing cover into proper position to supply lighting. Aerodynamic benefits were provided by this system only when the headlights were concealed.

In the 1960s, signal lamps and other special-purpose lights were increased in usage. Amber-colored front and red rear signal lights are flashed as a turn indication; all these lights are flashed simultaneously in the "flasher" system for use when a car is parked along a roadway or is traveling at a low speed on a high-speed highway. The law requires that marker lights that are visible from the front side and rear be also present. Red-colored that marker lights that are visible from the front side, and rear be also present. Red-colored rear signals are used to denotes braking, and on some models, cornering lamps to provide extra illumination in the direction of an intended turn are available. These are actuated in conjunction with the turn signals. To provide illumination to the rear when backing up, backup lights are required.

Unit 8 Engine Emission Control System

Part I Illustrated English

Diagram of Engine Emission System

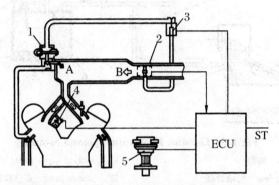

Fig. 8-1 Electronically Controlled Exhaust Gas Recirculation

1. EGR valve 废气再循环阀
2. EGR solenoid valve 废气再循环电磁阀
3. throttle 节气门
4. coolant temperature sensor 冷却液温度传感器
5. crankshaft position sensor 曲轴位置传感器
A. exhaust gas 排气
B. air 空气

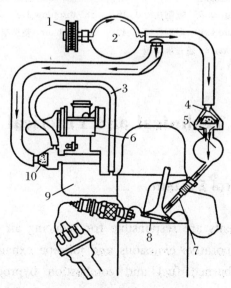

Fig. 8-2 EGR Solenoid Valve

1. air filter 空气滤清器
2. air pump 空气泵
3. prevent tempering pipe 防回火管
4. one-way valve 单向阀
5. air distribution pipe 空气分配管
6. carburetor 化油器
7. air nozzle 空气喷嘴
8. exhaust valve 排气门
9. intake pipe 进气管
10. tempering prevention valve 防回火阀

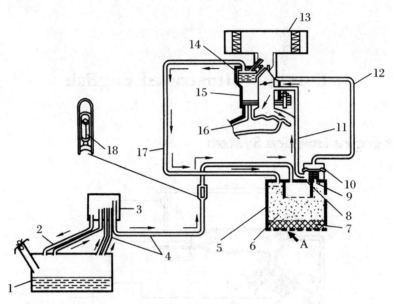

Fig. 8-3 Gasoline Evaporation Control System

1. fuel tank 油箱
2. oil return line 回油管路
3. oil and gas separator 油气分离器
4. gasoline vapor pipe 汽油蒸汽管
5. carbon canister 碳罐
6. activated carbon 活性炭
7. filter screen 过滤网
8. limiting aperture 0.76 限制孔径 0.76
9. limiting aperture 1.40 限制孔径 1.40
10. flow limiting valve 流量限制阀
11. gasoline vapor pipe 汽油蒸汽管
12. vacuum hose 真空软管
13. air filter 空气滤清器
14. float chamber 浮子室
15. carburetor 化油器
16. intake manifold 进气歧管
17. gasoline vapor pipe 汽油蒸汽管
18. throttle valve 节气门阀
A. fresh air 新鲜空气

Part Ⅱ Technical and Practical Reading

Engine Emission Control System

The vehicle components are responsible for reducing air pollution. This includes crankcase emissions, evaporative emissions and tailpipe exhaust emissions. Crankcase emissions consist of unburned fuel and combustion byproducts. These gases are recirculated back into the engine for reburning by the Positive Crankcase Ventilation

(PCV) system. Evaporative emissions are the fuel vapors that seep out of the fuel tank and carburetor. They are prevented from escaping into the atmosphere by sealing the fuel system and storing the vapors in a vapor canister for later reburning. Tailpipe exhaust emissions consist of carbon monoxide (CO), unburned hydrocarbons (HC) and oxides of nitrogen (NO_x). This formation of these pollutants is minimized by various engine design features, careful control over fuel calibration and ignition timing, and the EGR system. The pollutants that make it into the exhaust are "reburned" before they exit the tailpipe by the catalytic converter. The emission control system is an integral part of the engine, and should not be tampered with or disconnected. Devices related to the emission control system installed on the automobile are: tailpipe, muffler, EGR valve, catalytic converter, air pump, PCV valve, charcoal canister.

Catalytic Converter

Automotive emissions are controlled in three ways. One is to promote more complete combustion so that there are fewer byproducts. The second is to reintroduce excessive hydrocarbons back into the engine for combustion, and the third is to offer an additional area for oxidation or combustion to occur. This additional area is known as a catalytic converter. The catalytic converter looks like a muffler. It is located in the exhaust system ahead of the muffler. Inside the converter are pellets or a honeycomb made of platinum or palladium. The platinum or palladium is used as a catalyst (a catalyst is a substance used to speed up a chemical process). As hydrocarbons or carbon monoxide in the exhaust are passed over the catalyst, it is chemically oxidized converted to carbon dioxide and water. As the converter works to clean the exhaust, it develops heat. The dirtier the exhaust, the harder the converter works and the more heat that is developed. In some cases, the converter can be seen to glow from excessive heat. If the converter works too hard to clean a dirty exhaust, it will destroy itself. Also leaded fuel will put a coating on the platinum or palladium and render the converter ineffective.

PCV Valve

The purpose of the Positive Crankcase Ventilation (PCV) system produced in the crankcase during the normal combustion process, and redirecting them into the air-fuel intake system to be burned during combustion. These vapors dilute the air-fuel mixture, they need to be carefully controlled and metered so as not to affect the performance of the engine. This is the job of the Positive Crankcase Ventilation (PCV) valve. At idle, when the air-fuel mixture is very critical, just a few of the vapors are allowed into the intake system. At high speed when the mixture becomes less critical and the pressure in the engine is greater, more of the vapors are allowed into the intake system. When the valve or the system is clogged, vapors will back up into the air filter housing or at worst. The excess pressure will push past seals and create engine oil leaks. If the wrong valve is used or the system has air leaks, the engine will idle rough, or at worst engine oil will be sucked out of the engine.

EGR Valve

The purpose of the Exhaust Gas Recirculation (EGR) valve is to meter a small amount of exhaust gas into the intake system. This dilutes the air/fuel mixture so as to lower the combustion chamber temperature. Excessive combustion chamber temperature creates oxides of nitrogen, which is a major pollutant. While the EGR valve is the most effective method of controlling oxides of nitrogen, it adversely affects engine performance. The engine was not designed to run on exhaust gas. For this reason, the amount of exhaust entering the intake system needs to be carefully monitored and controlled and the vehicle computer. Since EGR action reduces performance by diluting the air-fuel mixture, the system doesn't allow EGR action when the engine is cold or when the engine needs full power.

Evaporative Controls

Gasoline evaporates quite easily. In the past, these evaporative emissions were vented into the atmosphere. 20% of all HC emissions from the automobile are from the gas tank. In 1970, legislation was passed, prohibiting venting of gas tank fumes into the atmosphere. An evaporative control system was designed to eliminate this source of pollution. The function of the fuel evaporative control system is to trap and store evaporative emissions from the gas tank and carburetor. A charcoal canister is used to trap the fuel vapors. The fuel vapors adhere to the charcoal, until the engine is started, and engine vacuum can be used to draw the vapors into the engine, so that they can be burned along with the fuel-air mixture. This system requires the use of a sealed gas tank filler cap. This cap is so important to the operation of the system that a test of the cap is now being integrated into many state emission inspection programs. Pre-1970 cars released fuel vapors into the atmosphere through the use of a vented gas cap. Today with the use of sealed caps, redesigned gas tanks are used. The tank has to have the space for the vapors to collect so that they can then be vented to the charcoal canister. A purge valve is used to control the vapor flow into the engine. The purge valve is operated by engine vacuum. One common problem with this system is that the purge valve goes bad and engine vacuum draws fuel directly into the intake system. This enriches the fuel mixture and will foul the spark plugs. Most charcoal canisters have a filter that should be replaced periodically. This system should be checked when fuel mileage drops.

Air Injection

Since no internal combustion engine is 100% efficient, there will always be some unburned fuel in the exhaust. This increases hydrocarbon emissions. To eliminate this source of emissions, an air injection system was created. Combustion requires fuel, oxygen and heat. Without any one of the three, combustion cannot occur. Inside the

Unit 8 Engine Emission Control System

exhaust manifold, there is sufficient heat to support combustion. If we introduce some oxygen, then any unburned fuel will ignite. This combustion will not produce any power, but it will reduce excessive hydrocarbon emissions. Unlike in the combustion chamber, this combustion is uncontrolled, so if the fuel content of the exhaust is excessive explosions that sound like popping will occur. There are times when under normal conditions, such as deceleration, when the fuel content is excessive. Under these conditions we would want to shut off the air injection system. This is accomplished through the use of a diverter valve, which instead of shutting the air pump off, diverts the air away from the exhaust manifold. Since all of this is done after the combustion process is complete, this is one emission control that has no effect on engine performance. The only maintenance that is required is a careful inspection of the air pump drive belt.

New Words

1. tailpipe ['telˌpaɪp] n. 排气管
2. byproduct ['baɪˌprɑdəkt] n. 副产品
3. seep [sip] v.（液体等）渗漏
4. canister ['kænɪstɚ] n.（放咖啡、茶叶、烟等的）小罐, 筒
5. reburn [riː'bɜːn] v. 再燃烧
6. pollutant [pə'lutnːt] n. 污染物
7. feature ['fitʃɚ] n. 特征
8. hydrocarbon [ˌhaɪdrə'kɑːrbən] n. [化学]烃, 碳氢化合物
9. calibration [ˌkæləˈbreʃən] n. 刻度, 核定
10. integral ['ɪntɪgrəl] adj. 整体的, 完整的
11. tamper ['tæmpɚ] v. 篡改, 玩弄
12. muffler ['mʌflɚ] n. 消音器
13. reintroduce [ˌriːɪntrə'duːs] v. 再引入, 再提出
14. oxidation [ˌɑksɪ'deʃən] n. [化学]氧化
15. pellet ['pɛlɪt] n. 小球
16. honeycomb ['hʌnikoʊm] n. 蜂窝
17. platinum ['plætnəm] n. 白金
18. palladium [pə'leɪdɪrm] n. [化学]钯
19. catalyst ['kæteɪst] n. 催化剂
20. glow [gloʊ] v. 发光, 发热
21. dirty ['dɜːrti] adj. 肮脏的
22. coating ['koʊtɪŋ] n. （薄的）覆盖层; 涂层
23. dilute [daɪ'lut, dɪ-] v. 稀释
24. clog [klɑːg] v. 阻塞障碍
25. rough [rʌf] adj./adv. 粗暴的, 粗暴地; 粗糙地
26. adversely [əd'vɜːslɪ] adv. 逆地, 相反地
27. performance [pər'fɔːrməns] n. 性能
28. monitor ['mɑːnɪtə(r)] v. 监听, 监控; 追踪, 检验
29. legislation [ˌlɛdʒɪ'sleʃən] n. 立法, 法规
30. fume [fjum] v. 愤怒, 冒烟
31. trap [træp] v. 使受限制
32. charcoal ['tʃɑːrkoʊl] n. 木炭
33. foul [faʊl] v. 弄脏
34. oxygen ['ɑːksɪdʒən] n. 氧
35. deceleration [ˌdiːsələ'reɪʃn] n. 减速
36. divert [daɪ'vɜːrt] v. 使转向

Phrases and Expressions

1. be responsible for 对……有责任的
2. PCV 曲轴箱强制通风装置
3. carbon monoxide 一氧化碳
4. ignition timing 点火正时
5. EGR 废气再循环装置
6. catalytic converter 催化转化器
7. speed up 加速
8. back up 倒退
9. at worst 在最坏的情况下
10. run on 涉及
11. exhaust gas 排气,废气
12. gas tank 汽油箱
13. here to 至此,到这里
14. filler cap （汽油箱）加油口盖
15. purge valve 排污阀
16. air injection 空气喷射
17. exhaust manifold 排气歧管
18. diverter valve 分流网
19. drive belt 传动皮带

Notes to Text

1. The dirtier the exhaust, the harder the converter works and the more heat that is developed.

尾气中所含碳氢化合物和一氧化碳的成分越多,净化器工作的难度就越大,并且产生的热量就越多。

2. These vapors dilute the air-fuel mixture, they have to be carefully controlled and metered so as not to affect the performance of the engine.

曲轴箱里的蒸汽可稀释可燃混合物,因此蒸汽的量必须要认真控制和测定,以免影响发动机的性能。

3. 20% of all HC emissions from the automobile are from the tank.

汽车排放物中的碳氢化合物的20%是来自于汽油箱。

4. The only maintenance that is required is a careful inspection of the air pump drive belt.

唯一要做的检修是认真检查空气泵的传动皮带。

Exercises

1. Answer the following questions to the text.

(1) What do crankcase emissions consist of?
(2) What are tailpipe exhaust emissions?
(3) How does a catalytic converter work?
(4) Why is the PCV valve used in an automobile?
(5) How does the EGR valve work?

2. Translate the following phrases and expressions into Chinese.

(1) emission control system

(2) positive crankcase ventilation system

(3) exhaust gas recirculation

(4) gas tank

(5) purge valve

(6) diverter valve

3. Translate the following sentences into Chinese.

(1) Devices related to the emission control system installed on the automobile are: tailpipe, muffler, EGR valve, catalytic converter, air pump, PCV valve, charcoal canister.

(2) The platinum or palladium is used as a catalyst (a catalyst is a substance used to speed up a chemical process).

(3) Excessive combustion chamber temperature creates oxides of nitrogen, which is a major pollutant.

(4) The function of the fuel evaporative control system is to trap and store evaporative emissions from the gas tank and carburetor.

(5) Since all of this is done after the combustion process is complete, this is one emission control that has no effect on engine performance.

(6) As hydrocarbons or carbon monoxide in the exhaust are passed over the catalyst. It is chemically oxidized or converted to carbon dioxide and water.

Part Ⅲ Listening and Speaking

Automotive Outsourcing A

A—Mr. Ford   B—Mr. Harper

A: Mr. Harper, I'd like to discuss with you about the problem of assembling dashboard for our newly launched car.

B: That's what I'm interested in, Mr. Ford.

A: I want to know if there is any tax exemption or reduction.

B: Yes, the tax exemption or reduction will allow you at least 5% more profit.

A: That's very attractive. Are you interested in the assembling business?

B: Yes, we're very much interested in your proposal that you supply us with an assembly line, technical information, and complete sets of component parts for us to assemble them into finished products.

A: That's fine. Let's come to the technical matters. We provide you with materials, components, necessary equipment and tools as well as the relevant technical data and blueprint needed for the assembling, and you should assemble strictly finished products according to the design specified by us without making any alteration.

B: You shall deliver the supplied materials and components to our warehouse. And the supplied assembly tools shall be reinstated at this end to ensure that they correspond to standards. Besides, if supplied materials do not conform to the requirements of the assembling, we shall ask you to send us replacements.

A: That sounds reasonable. How long would you like to make a contract with us?

B: Three years.

A: Acceptable. We'd like to know your rate of assembling charges.

B: The assembling charge for each set are 15 dollars and the payment is to be made by sight L/C to be opened by you not later than 30 days before shipment.

A: OK.

B: Well, there's one thing you might need to know. After this contract is signed, you shall send at your own expense 5 technicians to our plant to render technical assistance during assembling and to inspect the finished products before delivery.

A: Yes. I think we have settled all the points under dispute. Mr. Harper, I hope we will cooperate with each other very well.

Automotive Outsourcing B

A—Mr. Mitchel   B—Mr. Judd

A: Mr. Judd, would you like to enter into a processing contract for assembly with us?

B: Yes, what type of products do you intend to assemble?

A: Seats for our new types of car.

B: We have set up an automatic assembly line for seats in all model of car. So your suggestion is very attractive. Please tell me something about it in detail, Mr. Mitchel.

A: We hope you process and assemble for us 20,000 seats for light truck and 20,000 for medium truck within a period of two years, and all necessary parts and components will be supplied by us.

B: What's the assembling fee for each set?

A: The assembling charge for each set is 50 yuan RMB.

B: 50 yuan? But 60 yuan is our minimum.

A: Even though 60 yuan is very harsh on us, we accept.

B: What's the method of payment?

A: We shall pay you by opening an irrevocable L/C covering the full amount of assembling charges. You shall complete the assembling of all seats and effect shipment within the contracted time unless some unforeseen circumstances beyond control have occured.

B: Well, it sounds reasonable. What do you consider about the damage rate of parts and components?

A: The damage rate for parts and components in assembling is 2%, which is the rate of spare parts and components to be supplied free by us. In case the damage rate exceeds 2%, you shall provide at your own expense for the excessive shortage of parts and components needed for assembling.

B: 2% is too small. As you know, 3% is the international practice.

A: Um ... Well, for the long-term relationship in the future, we agree to accept 3%.

B: If you fail to supply the components in time, all losses incurred will be paid by you.

A: Yes, but if you fail to deliver seats in time, all losses thus incurred will be paid by you. Shipment of finished seats shall be done once a month.

B: OK, we agree. When we have any difficulties, you shall dispatch technicians to our plant to help training technicians and allow the technicians to remain with us for inspection of finished products. In such a case, we shall pay monthly salary 1,000 yuan RMB for each person. All other expenses, including round trip tickets, shall be paid by you.

A: No problem. I'm very pleased that we have come to an agreement at last.

Part IV   Reading Material

Vehicle emission control in China

Advanced technologies should be incorporated in auto design to reduce exhaust emissions, according to an article in *China Economic Times*. An excerpt are as follows.

The State Environmental Protection Administration estimates that by 2005 about 79 percent of all air pollution will come from automobile exhaust emissions. And urban air pollution will shift from the current combination of coal smoke exhaust to mainly auto exhaust.

The country's large-scale auto emission pollution can be attributed to the backward standard of controls. In 2001, China adopted the first standard of exhaust emission, equivalent to the Euro I, 20 years later than developed countries. And the second standard, equivalent to the Euro II, was instituted in 2003—eight years later than developed nations. The current schedule calls for adopting the Euro III standard between 2008 and 2010, still eight years later. The delay in adopting international emission standards has led to high fuel consumption, the low fuel utilization and rampant emissions from made-in-China autos.

There is a huge gap between the technologies of emission control and engine production in China and those of the developed countries.

In addition, due to lack of strict supervision in the management of obsolete autos, many of these vehicles have entered the market and continue to run on the road.

For effectively controlling exhaust emission pollution, China should try to master advanced technologies as quickly as possible. The Euro III and IV standards adhere to advanced system, taking into account fuel quality, road condition, and transportation management, driving technique and habit and daily car maintenance. Some joint ventures have already mastered such technology. Domestic enterprises should speed up the pace of their research and development in this aspect. Measures should also be taken to accelerate the discard of old cars.

Meanwhile, preferential tax policies should be allowed to encourage consumers to purchase low polluters.

Exhaust pollution should not be an obstacle to the growth of China's auto industry, once effective measures and advanced technologies are implemented.

Unit 9 Engine Cooling System

Part I Illustrated English

Diagram of Engine Cooling System

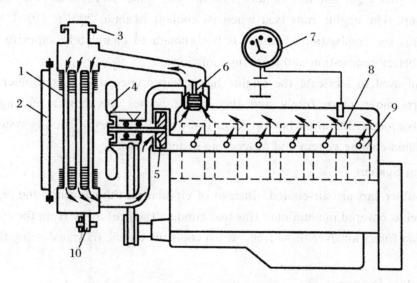

Fig. 9-1 Forced Circulating Liquid Cooling System

1. shutter 百叶窗
2. radiator 散热器
3. radiator cap 散热器盖
4. cooling fan 冷却风扇
5. water pump 水泵
6. thermostat 节温器
7. coolant temperature indicator 冷却液温度表
8. water jacket 水套
9. distributive pipe 分水管
10. drain valve 放水阀

Part II Technical and Practical Reading

Engine Cooling System

Although gasoline engines have improved a lot, they are still not very efficient at turning chemical energy into mechanical power. Most of the energy in the gasoline (perhaps 70%) is converted into heat, and it is the job of the cooling system to take care of that heat. In fact, the cooling system on a car driving down the freeway dissipates enough heat to heat two average-sized houses. The primary job of the cooling system is to keep the engine from overheating by transferring this heat to the air, but the cooling system also has several other important jobs. When the engine is cold, components wear out faster, and the engine is less efficient and emits more pollution. So another important job of the cooling system is to allow the engine to heat up as quickly as possible, and then to keep engine at a constant temperature.

The Basics

Inside the car's engine, fuel is constantly burning. A lot of the heat from this combustion goes right out the exhaust system, but some of it soaks into the engine, heating it up. The engine runs best when its coolant is about 200 °F (93 °C). At this temperature, the combustion chamber is hot enough to completely vaporize the fuel, providing better combustion and reducing emissions.

The oil used to lubricate the engine has a lower viscosity (it is thinner), so the engine parts move more freely and the engine wastes less power moving its own components around. Metal parts wear less. There are two types of cooling systems found on cars: liquid-cooling system and air-cooling system.

Air Cooling System

Some older cars are air-cooled. Instead of circulating fluid through the engine, the engine block is covered in aluminum fins that conduct the heat away from the cylinder. A powerful fan forces air over these fins, which cools the engine by transferring the heat to the air.

Liquid Cooling System

Now, most cars are liquid-cooled. The cooling system on liquid-cooled cars circulates a fluid through pipes and passageways in the engine. As this liquid passes through the hot engine, it absorbs heat, cooling the engine. After the fluid leaves the engine, it passes through a heat exchanger, or radiator, which transfers the heat from the fluid to the air blowing through the exchanger.

Plumbing

The cooling system in your car has a lot of plumbing. The pump sends the fluid into the engine block, where it makes its way through passages in the engine around the cylinders. Then it returns through the cylinder head of the engine. The thermostat is located where the fluid leaves the engine. The plumbing ground the thermostat sends the fluid back to the pump directly if the thermostat is closed. If it is open, the fluid goes through the radiator first and then back to the pump.

Fluid

Cars operate in a wide variety of temperatures, from well below freezing to well over 100°F (38 °C). So whatever fluid is used to cool the engine, it has to have a very low freezing point, a high boiling point, and it has to have the capacity to hold a lot of heat.

Water is one of the most effective fluid for holding heat, but water freezes at too high a temperature to be used in car engines. The fluid that most cars use is a mixture of water and ethylene glycol ($C_2H_6O_2$), also known as antifreeze. By adding ethylene glycol to water, the boiling and freezing points are improved significantly.

The temperature of the coolant can sometimes reach 250 °F to 275 °F (121 °C to 135 °C). Even with ethylene glycol added, these temperatures would boil the coolant, so something additional must be done to raise its boiling point.

The cooling system uses pressure to further raise the boiling point of the coolant. Just as the boiling temperature of water is higher in a pressure cooker, the boiling temperature of coolant is higher if you pressurize the system. Most cars have a pressure limit of 14 to 15 pounds per square inch (psi), which raises the boiling point another 45 °F (25 °C) so the coolant can withstand the high temperature. Antifreeze also contains additives to resist corrosion.

Water Pump

The water pump is a simple centrifugal pump driven by a belt connected to the crankshaft of the engine. The pump circulates fluid whenever the engine is running. The water pump uses centrifugal force to send fluid to the outside while it spins, causing fluid to be drawn from the center continuously. The inlet to the pump is located near the center so that fluid returning from the radiator hits the pump vanes. The pump vanes flying the fluid to the outside of the pump, where it can enter the engine. The fluid leaving the pump flows first through the engine block and cylinder head, then into the radiator and finally back to the pump. The engine block and cylinder head have many passageways cast or machined in them to allow for fluid flow. These passageways direct the coolant to the most critical areas of the engine.

Radiator

A radiator is a type of heat exchanger. It is designed to transfer heat from the hot coolant that flows through it to the air blown through it by the fan.

Most modern cars use aluminum radiators. These radiators are made by brazing thin aluminum fins to flattened aluminum tubes. The coolant flows from the inlet to the outlet through many tubes mounted in a parallel arrangement. The fins conduct the heat from the tubes and transfer it to the air flowing through the radiator. The tubes sometimes have a type of fin inserted into them called a turbulator, which increases the turbulence of the fluid flowing through the tubes. If the fluid flowed very smoothly through the tubes, only the fluid actually touching the tubes would be cooled directly. The amount of heat transferred to the tubes from the fluid running through them depends on the difference in temperature between the tube and the fluid touching it. So if the fluid that is in contact with the tube cools down quickly, less heat will be transferred. By creating turbulence inside the tube, all of the fluid mixes together, keeping the temperature of the fluid touching the tubes up so that more heat can be extracted, and all of the fluid inside the tube is used effectively.

Radiator Cap

The radiator cap actually increases the boiling point of your coolant by about 45 ℉ (25 ℃). How does this simple cap do this? The same way a pressure cooker increases the boiling temperature of water. The cap is actually a pressure release valve, and on cars it is usually set to 15 psi. The boiling point of water increases when the water placed under pressure. When the fluid in the cooling system heats up, it expands, causing the pressure to build up. The cap is the only place where this pressure can escape, so the setting of the spring on the cap determines the maximum pressure in the cooling system. When the pressure reaches 15 psi, the pressure pushes the valve open, allowing coolant to escape from the cooling system. This coolant flows through the overflow tube into the bottom of the overflow tank. This arrangement keeps air out of the system. When the radiator cools back down, a vacuum is created in the cooling system that pulls another spring loaded valve open, sucking water back in from the bottom of the overflow tank to replace the water that was expelled.

Thermostat

The thermostat's main job is to allow the engine to heat up quickly, and then to keep the engine at a constant temperature. It does this by regulating the amount of water that goes through the radiator. At low temperature, the outlet to the radiator is completely blocked. Once the temperature of the coolant rises to between 180 ℉ and 195 ℉ (82 ℃ ~91 ℃), the thermostat starts to open, allowing fluid to flow through the radiator. By the time the coolant reaches 200 ℉ to 218 ℉ (93 ℃~103 ℃), the thermostat is open all the way.

The secret of the thermostat lies in the small cylinder located on the engine-side of the device. This cylinder is filled with a wax that begins to melt at around 180 ℉ (different thermostats open at different temperature, but 180 ℉ is a common one). A rod connected to the valve presses into this wax. When the wax melts, it expands significantly, pushing the rod out of the cylinder and opening the valve.

Fan

Like the thermostat, the cooling fan has to be controlled so that it allows the engine to maintain a constant temperature.

Front-wheel drive cars have electric fans because the engine is usually mounted transversely, meaning the output of the engine points toward the side of the car. The fans are controlled either with a thermostatic switch or by the engine computer, and they turn on when the temperature of the coolant goes above a set point. They turn back off when the temperature drops below that point.

Rear-wheel drive cars with longitudinal engines usually have engine-driven cooling fans. These fans have a thermostatically controlled viscous clutch. This clutch is positioned at the hub of the fan, in the airflow coming through the radiator. This special viscous clutch is much like the viscous coupling sometimes found in all-wheel drive cars.

New Words

1. dissipate ['dɪsɪpet] v. （使）驱散，浪费
2. primary ['praɪməri] adj. 主要的
3. out [aʊt] adv. 明显地
4. overheat [ˌəʊvə'hiːt] vt. 使过热
5. wear [wɛə] vi. 磨损
6. emit [ɪ'mɪt] v. 放射（光热，味等）
7. soak [səʊk] v. 吸收，吸入
8. Fahrenheit ['færən'haɪt] n. 华氏温度的
9. Celsius ['sɛlsɪəs] adj. 摄氏的
10. vaporize ['vepə'raɪz] vt./vi. （使）蒸发
11. viscosity [vɪs'kɒsɪti] n. 黏度，黏性
12. aluminum [ə'lʊmɪnəm] n. 铝
13. fin [fɪn] n. 散热片
14. conduct [kən'dʌkt] v. 传导
15. transfer [træns'fɜː] vt. 传递，转移
16. circulate ['sɜːkjʊleɪt] v. 使循环，循环
17. fluid ['fluːɪd] n. 液体
18. passageway ['pæsɪdʒɪweɪ] n. 通路，通道
19. radiator ['reɪdɪˌeɪtə] n. 散热器
20. plumbing ['plʌmɪŋ] n. 水管装置
21. pump [pʌmp] n. 泵，抽水机
22. thermostat ['θɜːməˌstæt] n. 节温器
23. separate ['seprət] v. 独立
24. antifreeze ['æntɪfriz] n. 防冻剂
25. significant [sɪg'nɪfɪkənt] adj. 重大的，重要的
26. additional [ə'dɪʃənl] adj. 附加的
27. cooker ['kʊkə] n. 厨具，厨灶
28. withstand [wɪð'stænd] v. 承受；抵制
29. additive ['ædətɪv] n. 添加剂
30. resist [rɪ'zɪst] v. 反抗，抵制
31. corrosion [kə'rəʊʒən] n. 腐蚀
32. centrifugal [sɛn'trɪfjʊgəl] adj. 离心的
33. spin [spɪn] v. 自转
34. vane [ven] n. 叶片，轮片
35. fling [flɪŋ] v. 抛，掷
36. coolant ['kʊlənt] n. 冷却剂
37. critical ['krɪtɪkl] adj. 关键的
38. braze [breɪz] v. 用黄铜镀或制造
39. flatten ['flætən] v. 弄平，变平
40. turbulence ['tɜːbjʊləns] n. （水流的）汹涌
41. suck [sʌk] v. 吮吸，吸取
42. wax [wæks] v. 蜡，打蜡
43. transverse [trænz'vɜːs] adj. 横向的
44. longitudinal [ˌlɒndʒɪ'tjuːdɪnəl] adj. 纵向的
45. fan [fæn] n. 风扇
46. clutch [klʌtʃ] n. 离合器

Phrases and Expressions

1. cooling system　制冷系统
2. mechanical power　机械功
3. heat exchanger　热交换机
4. air-cooled　风冷的
5. liquid-cooled　液体冷却的
6. freezing point　冰点
7. boiling point　沸点
8. ethylene glycol　甘醇,乙二醇
9. regardless of　不管,不顾
10. water pump　水泵
11. radiator cap　散热器盖
12. as quickly as possible　尽可能快地
13. heat up　加热
14. keep ... from　阻止,使免于
15. take care of　处理,清除

Notes to Text

1. When the engine is cold, components wear out faster, and the engine is less efficient and emits more pollution.
当发动机低温运行时,零部件磨损得更快,并且发动机的工作效率将降低,同时释放出更多的污染物。

2. The fluid that most cars use is a mixture of water and ethylene glycol ($C_2H_6O_2$), also known as antifreeze.
大多数车辆所使用的冷却液体是一种水和乙二醇的混合物,这种混合物也被称为防冻剂。

3. The engine block and cylinder head have many passageways cast or machined in them to allow for fluid flow.
在发动机缸体和缸盖里有许多铸造或者机械加工成的通道,可用来让冷却剂流动。

4. The amount of heat transferred to the tubes from the fluid running through them depends on the difference in temperature between the tube and the fluid touching it.
流过管子的制冷液传递热量的多少取决于管子和流经它的制冷液之间的温差。

5. The fans are controlled either with a thermostatic switch or by the engine computer, and they turn on when the temperature of the coolant goes above a set point.
风扇既可以被节温器上的开关控制,又可以被发动机上的计算机控制。当制冷剂的温度超过规定温度时,风扇转动。

Exercises

1. Answer the following questions to the text.

(1) What is the primary job of the cooling system?
(2) Explain two types of cooling systems found on cars, please.
(3) How does the thermostat work?
(4) Why is there a radiator in the cooling system?

(5) What is the function of the water pump?

2. Translate the following phrases and expressions into Chinese.

(1) mechanical power

(2) liquid-cooled engine

(3) radiator cap

(4) ethylene glycol

(5) regardless of

(6) boiling point

3. Translate the following sentences into Chinese.

(1) The primary job of the cooling system is to keep the engine from overheating by transferring this heat to the air, but the cooling system also has several other important jobs.

(2) At this temperature, the combustion chamber is hot enough to completely vaporize the fuel, providing better combustion and reducing emissions.

(3) Some older cars are air-cooled. Instead of circulating fluid through the engine, the engine block is covered in aluminum fins that conduct the heat away from the cylinder.

(4) After the fluid leaves the engine, it passes through a heat exchanger, or radiator, which transfers the heat from the fluid to the air blowing through the exchanger.

(5) The water pump is a simple centrifugal pump driven by a belt connected to the crankshaft of the engine.

(6) The fans are controlled either with a thermostatic switch or by the engine computer, and they turn on when the temperature of the coolant goes above a set point.

Part Ⅲ Listening and Speaking

Production Supervision A

A—Porter   B—Miss Kim

A: Good afternoon, Miss Kim. I'm Porter. I'm responsible for the work done at the factory.

B: Good afternoon, Porter. Your factory looks very busy.

A: It is. It's peak season now and we are working at full capacity. Our factory has a production capacity of thirty thousands per year.

B: Then what does your factory produce?

A: We manufacture automobiles. Some of the spare parts are hand-made and some are machine-made.

B: Does your company carry out the entire process of manufacturing?

A: Of course not. We usually ask a few smaller factories to make the parts required and then our designing section assembles the item. These accessories are made by outside factories which specialize in this kind of work.

B: What kind of quality control do you have, since some of your spare parts are produced by other factories?

A: Well, there is no need to worry about the quality. You know that quality is our company's primary consideration. All products have to go through five checks during the manufacturing process. And the entire manufacturing process is under our supervision.

B: Well, thank you for showing me your plant and answering my questions patiently. In fact, your company impressed me a lot.

Production Supervision B

A—Sales Manager   B—Mr. William

A: Mr. William, you have been to our exhibition. What items are you particularly interested in this time?

B: I'm very interested in your latest racing model. They look smart, but I want to know some distinguishing features of these racing cars.

A: Mr. William, you have good taste. These racing cars are our competitive products, and they are well-received with the young people. As for its distinguishing features, the new product is different in many ways—design, material. It's more solidly built and in better finish.

B: What about safety features?

A: Well, take the air-conditioner in the racing car for example. It has an automatic thermostat control which keeps temperatures from reaching unsafe levels.

B: Your company used to have trouble with quality control. Can you tell me how your company insures that your latest model meet a uniform high standard?

A: We know that the high quality of the products will secure the leading status in the market place. So we have a very strict quality controlling system which promises that the automobiles we produced are always of the best quality. Specifically speaking, at first, we had to station one of our engineers at the factories we used to forge the spare parts for our racing cars. But by now these factories have stringent quality control of their own.

B: I'm impressed a lot by the modern facilities and diligent workers in the plant.

A: It's nice of you to say so.

Part Ⅳ   Reading Material

Air Conditioner

Not only do we depend on our cars to get us where we want to go, we also depend on them to get us there without discomfort. We expect the heater to get us warm when it is cold outside, and the air conditioning system to keep us cool when it is hot.

The main parts of the air conditioning system are the compressor, the condenser, the receiver or the accumulator, the cooling unit (with an evaporator and an expansion valve in it), the heater unit and the heater control assembly, blow unit, A/C control ECU, suction hose and discharge hose, and necessary hoses and sensors, etc.

Like your body, the air conditioning compressor is the heart of the AC system, and Freon is the blood. This Freon is a gas and liquid combination that is compressed and circulated throughout the air conditioning system. The compressor pumps Freon throughout the AC system, either the older type R12 which costs as much as gold it seems these days, or the new environmentally-friendly R134A Freon. R12 is extremely dangerous. It is believed to cause harm by depleting the ozone which helps to protect us from the ultraviolet from the sun. However, R134A doesn't deplete the ozone, and its evaporative temperature is -26.4 ℃, higher than that of R12. The compressed Freon is pushed through the system under pressure and is passed through different sized metal and rubber hoses and a special valve called an expansion valve that causes the gas to expand and contract.

This expansion and contraction makes the Freon gas very cold. This cold gas makes its way via metal lines into the dash area of your vehicle to the evaporator core. This evaporator core is like a small radiator, except it has cold Freon circulating inside and not hot antifreeze. A small fan (the AC blower fan which you control from the control panel on the dash) sit in front of the evaporator core and blows air across this cold evaporator and then through the vents inside your vehicle.

The heat is removed by the Freon with the help of the AC condenser located at the front of the car (usually in front of the radiator). The Freon coming back from die evaporator carries the heat from the cab to the condenser via rubber and metal hoses. Just like your radiator, the condenser is lightweight aluminum with many internal winding coils. The Freon travels through these coils, and in between these coils are small slits or fins that the Freon is forced through. The condenser will have an electric cooling fan mounted in front or behind it to push or pull air through these fins to remove the heat from the Freon. Some vehicles still use the old fashioned fan blade driven by the engine to pull air across the radiator and the condenser.

There are a few causes of low cooling efficiency or no cooling at all at idle.

Lack of Air Flow Across the Condenser

Make sure the electric cooling fan motor near the condenser is coming on, or in models that are equipped with a fan blade make sure this fan turning and is turning very fast.

Low Freon Levels

Freon level and pressure should be checked by your certified air conditioning mechanic.

Overheating

If the engine is running hot or overheating, it can have a noticeable negative effect on the air conditioning system. Some cars have two electric cooling fans, one for the air conditioning condenser and the other for the radiator. Make sure they are both working properly. Usually at idle on a hot day with the AC on both fans will be on. When the vehicle is traveling at freeway speed, the compressor is pumping the Freon throughout the system much faster and harder than at idle. There is a dramatic increase in air flow across the condenser due to 55 mph winds, and the engine is usually operating at a cooler more efficient temperature as well, thus allowing the air conditioning system to operate efficiently.

An air conditioning system that is somewhat low on Freon can still feel comfortable at freeway speed due to the added air flow across the condenser which can overcome the ill effects of slightly low Freon. Periodic air conditioning performance checks by your mechanic are the best way to keep the system in great shape.

Unit 10 Engine Lubricating System

Part I Illustrated English

Diagram of Engine Lubricating System

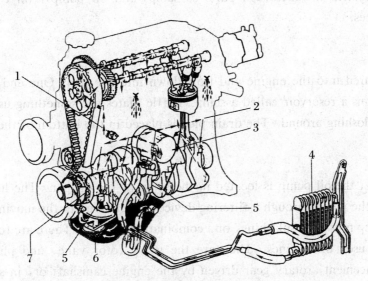

Fig. 10-1 Lubricating System

1. oil pressure switch 机油压力开关
2. mail oil gallery 主油道
3. oil filter 机油滤清器
4. oil cooler 机油冷却器
5. relief valve 泄压阀
6. oil strainer 机油收集器
7. oil pump 机油泵

Part II Technical and Practical Reading

Engine Lubricating System

The reliability and performance of modern engines are directly dependent on the effectiveness of their lubricating systems. To be effective, an engine lubricating system must successfully perform the functions of minimizing friction between the bearing surfaces of moving parts, dissipating heat, and keeping the engine parts clean by removing carbon and other foreign matter. In almost all modern internal combustion engines, the system that provides the oil for these functions is the forced lubrication type of design. Although there are many variations in lubricating systems for internal combustion engines, the components and method of operation are basically the same for all designs.

The lubricating system of an internal combustion engine consists of two main divisions. One is inside the engine, the other is outside the engine. The internal system consists mainly of passages and piping. The external system includes several components which aid in supplying the oil in the proper quantity, at the proper temperature, and free of impurities. In the majority of lubricating oil systems for internal-combustion engines, the external system includes such parts as sumps and oil pumps, oil coolers and oil filtering devices.

Sump

Oil is poured into the engine and flow down into the pan. One end of the pan is lower and forms a reservoir called a sump. Baffle plates are something used to prevent the oil from sloshing around. The drain plug is placed in the bottom of the sump.

Pumps

Generally, the oil pump is located in the sump of the oil pan. The lubricating oil, which enters the pump through a filtering device, is delivered to the moving parts of the engine by pump pressure, splashing, or a combination of both. There are four main types of oil pumps used on engines. They are the gear, rotor vane, and plunger pumps. Positive displacement, rotary gear driven by the engine camshaft or, in some engines, directly by the crankshaft, the oil is supplied at flow rates adjusted to the needs of the engine. Changes in engine speed will cause corresponding changes in pump output.

The operating pressure is normally controlled by one or more pressure regulating valves, which open or close as necessary to maintain the specified flow rate to various load-bearing parts of the engine. These spring-actuated devices divert excess oil directly to the engine sump or back to the inlet of the lubricating oil sump.

Oil Coolers

The lubricating oil systems of most engines use coolers (heat exchangers) to maintain the oil temperature within the most efficient operating range. Oil, passing through the operating engine, absorbs heat from the metal parts. Since engine oil is recirculated and used over and over, it is continually absorbing additional heat. Unless the heat is removed, the oil temperature will rise to excessive values at extremely high temperature, oil tends to oxidize rapidly and form carbon deposits. Excessive engine operating temperature also causes and increases in the rate of oil consumption. Consequently, oil coolers are required to remove excess heat from the oil so that the oil will retain its lubricating qualities.

The coolers used to remove heat from lubricating oil are of the same type as those used to remove heat from other fluids common to internal combustion engines. These coolers are referred to as shell and tube, strut tube, or plate tube coolers.

Filtering Devices

Oil must be cleaned before it goes into the lubricating system of an engine. Oil must also be cleaned regularly while it is being recirculated through the engine. Dust and dirt particles from the intake air get into the oil system. Flakes of metal from the engine parts are also picked up and carried in the oil. Carbon particles from incomplete combustion in the cylinders work into the oil. Heat causes the oil itself to deteriorate and form sludge and gummy material which may coat load-bearing or heat-transfer surfaces, or circulate through the oil system. Some water will get into the oil, even when precautions are taken.

Strainers

Lubricating oil strainers may be either simplex or duplex. A duplex strainer is two strainer elements in one assembly. A manual valve directs the flow of oil through either of the elements. When duplex strainers are used, one element can be removed and cleaned without disturbing the flow of oil through the other element to the engine.

Filters

In filters approved by the Navy, the absorbent material is composed of such substances as cellulose, cotton yarn, and paper disks. Filters may be located directly in the pressure-lubricating oil system, or they may be installed as bypass filters. When installed in the pressure system, a filter must contain a built-in, spring-loaded, pressure-relief valve. The valve must be large enough to bypass all oil to the engine in case the element becomes restricted.

A bypass filter has an orifice plate in the line to the filter. This component controls the amount of oil removed from the lubricating oil pressure system. (The amount of oil that flows through a bypass filter is only a small percentage of the oil that flows through the pressure system.) The oil from a bypass filter is returned to the sump tank. Filters vary as much in design and construction as strainers.

A kind of satisfactory engine lubricating oil must have proper viscosity and must resist oxidation, carbon formation, corrosion, rust, extreme pressure, and foaming. Furthermore, it must act as a good cleaning agent, and must have good viscosity at extremely high or low temperature. But any mineral oil doesn't have all these properties by itself. So a number of additives are put into the oil during the progress of producing.

New Words

1. lubricating ['lu:brɪkeɪtɪŋ] adj. 润滑的
2. friction ['frɪkʃən] n. 摩擦,摩擦力
3. bearing ['berɪŋ] n. 轴承,举止,意义
4. dissipate ['dɪsəˌpet] v. (使)驱散,浪费
5. oil [ɔɪl] n. 机油,石油,润滑油
6. lubrication [ˌlubrɪ'keʃən] n. 润滑
7. component [kəm'poʊnənt] n. 部分,零件
8. division [dɪ'vɪʒən] n. 部分,片段
9. external [ɪk'stɜːrnl] adj. 外部的
10. passage ['pæsɪdʒ] n. 油路,通道
11. piping ['paɪpɪŋ] n. 管道
12. aid [ed] n. 帮助
13. impurity [ɪm'pjʊrəti] n. 不纯,杂质
14. strainer ['streɪnə] v. 滤网
15. slosh [slɑːʃ] v. 溅,泼
16. splash [splæʃ] v. 溅,飞溅
17. vane [ven] n. 叶片
18. crankcase ['kræŋkˌkeɪs] n. 曲轴箱
19. plunger ['plʌndʒə] n. 柱塞
20. deposit [dɪ'pɑːzɪt] vt./vi. 存放,堆积/沉淀
21. cooler ['kulə] n. 冷却器
22. oxidize ['ɑːksɪdaɪz] vt. 氧化
23. dust [dʌst] n. 尘土,粉末
24. flake [flek] n. 片,片状物
25. sludge [slʌdʒ] n. 污泥
26. abrasive [ə'bresɪv] n. 研磨剂,磨损颗粒
27. deteriorate [dɪ'tɪriəreɪt] v. 恶化,败坏
28. navy ['nevi] n. 海军
29. simplex ['sɪmpleks] adj. 单一的
30. duplex ['duːpleks] adj. 双倍的,复式的
31. bypass ['baɪˌpæs] v./n. 设旁路/迂回旁路
32. cellulose ['seljuloʊs] n. 植物纤维质,纤维素
33. yarn [jɑːrn] n. 纱线
34. mesh [mɛʃ] n. 网孔,筛眼
35. viscosity [vɪ'skɑsɪti] n. 黏度
36. foam [foʊm] n. 泡沫
37. rust [rʌst] n./v. 锈/生锈
38. corrosion [kə'roʒən] n. 腐蚀
39. additive ['ædɪtɪv] n. 添加剂

Phrases and Expressions

1. lubricating system 润滑系统
2. bearing surface 支撑表面,轴承工作面
3. forced lubrication 压力润滑法
4. drain plug 排污阀
5. oil pump 油泵
6. oil cooler 机油散热器
7. oil pan 油底壳
8. positive displacement 容积式
9. moving part 运动部件
10. pressure regulating valve 压力调节阀
11. flow rate 流速
12. heat exchanger 热交换器
13. over and over 反复,再三
14. lubricating oil 润滑油
15. heat-transfer surface 传热表面
16. pressure-relief valve 减压阀

Unit 10 Engine Lubricating System

Notes to Text

1. To be effective, an engine lubricating system must successfully perform the functions of minimizing friction between surfaces of moving parts, dissipating heat, and keeping the engine parts clean by moving carbon and other foreign matter.

为了让发动机的润滑系统能有效地工作,它必须要实现以下功能:把运动部件表面之间的摩擦力减到最小、散热以及通过清除碳和其他杂质使发动机各部分保持清洁。

2. The lubricating oil, which enters the pump through a filtering device, is delivered to the moving parts of the engine by pump pressure, splashing, or a combination of both.

通过过滤装置进入到机油泵的润滑油以油泵压力、激溅、复合等润滑方式输送到发动机的各个运动部件。

3. Heat causes the oil itself to deteriorate and form sludge and gummy material which may

   coat load-bearing or heat-transfer, or circulate through the oil system.

热量导致机油本身变质,形成淤泥和带有黏性的物质。这些物质可以覆盖在承重表面上,或者通过润滑系统循环掉。

4. A kind of satisfactory engine lubricating oil must have proper viscosity and must resist

   oxidation, carbon formation, corrosion, rust, extreme pressure, and foaming.

一种令人满意的发动机润滑油必须有适当的黏度,还必须具备抗氧化性、能防止碳的形成、耐腐蚀、能防止生锈以及耐高压和抗泡沫性。

Exercises

1. **Answer the following questions to the text.**

   (1) What is the function of the lubricating system?
   (2) Why is the filtering device installed on the engine?
   (3) Why is the additive put into the oil?
   (4) What is the most important property of the oil?
   (5) Where is the oil pump generally?

2. **Translate the following phrases and expressions into Chinese.**

   (1) moving part
   (2) lubricating system
   (3) drain plug
   (4) pressure-relief valve
   (5) pressure regulating valve
   (3) positive displacement

3. Translate the following sentences into Chinese.

(1) In the majority of lubricating oil systems for internal combustion engines, the external system includes such parts as sumps, oil pumps, oil coolers, and oil filtering devices.

(2) The lubricating oil, which enters the pup through a filtering device, is delivered to the moving parts of the engine by pump pressure, splashing, or a combination of both.

(3) Consequently, oil coolers are required to remove excess heat from the oil so that the oil will retain its lubricating qualities.

(4) Devices that have replaceable, absorbent cartridges are called filters.

(5) A satisfactory engine lubricating oil must have proper viscosity and must resist oxidation, carbon formation, corrosion rust, extreme pressure, and foaming.

(6) It must act as a good cleaning agent, and must have good viscosity at extremely high or low temperature.

Part Ⅲ Listening and Speaking

Production Safety A

A—Salesperson B—Customer

A: Good morning. Anything I can do for you?
B: I'd like to look at some of these cars.
A: We have various cars. Do you want a domestically made or an imported car?
B: A domestic car is cheaper than an imported one. So I'd prefer a domestic one.
A: OK. Please have a look over there.
B: I think I would like to see some cars with manual transmission.
A: Fine. What about the blue car? It is our latest model.
B: But I'd like the economy model better.
A: OK. How about the white one?
B: Let me think about it. Can I have a test drive?
A: Sure. This way, please.
B: I'm very satisfied with this white one, so shall we talk about the inspection of the cars?
A: Sure, Mr. Chen. The inspection of a commodity is an integral part of the contract. But as you know, we've gone through the inspection of cars before delivery. So do you think it is still necessary to have them reinspect the cars at the destination?
B: I'm afraid it is. It's a common practice in international trade today that the exporters

have the right to inspect goods before delivery, while the buyers have the right to reinspect the goods after their arrival.

A: Oh, Mr. Chen. I quite understand your situation on this point. So you have to engage a surveyor as soon as possible.

B: As a matter of fact, we've had the best surveyor, the China Import and Export Commodity Inspection Bureau, which has a prestigious fame all around the world.

A: OK, We'll try to complete the reinspection as soon as possible.

B: I hope there's no occasion for any disagreeable things to happen.

Production Safety B

A—David   B—Hanson

A: Across all industries a growing body of research indicates that workplace accidents are well under reported. Some employers pressure workers to avoid reporting safety hazards and accidents.

B: Since the Occupational Safety and Health Administration (OSHA) was created in 1790, the death rates from injuries have gone down.

A: OSHA has been successful in many different fronts. But OSHA has been so poorly supported by government and by the public. With their current budget and staffing, it would take OSHA 119 years to inspect every workplace. It is just not possible. Now, I don't think we would want an OSHA that is capable of going out and physically inspecting every workplace. We need employers to run their workplaces in a safe and health manner to begin with.

B: How frequently are criminal penalties imposed for employers exposing their workers to dangerous conditions?

A: I was looking recently to find out how many people actually received jail time for willful OSHA violations. I couldn't find one. I don't know if anybody has served any serious jail time for a workplace fatality.

B: You worked with companies as a safety officer. Why can't companies themselves assure a safe workplace?

A: Many can and many do. Many want to keep their workers safe and healthy. But as with anything, there are those that need more pressure to do things the right way. Sometimes it costs money. The threat of an inspection of a penalty helps push some employers — who may choose to take a short cut — to do the right thing.

B: Do the majority of employers want to do the right thing?

A: I would hope so, yes.

B: They know that a strong OSHA helps them do the right thing. Why don't the businesses organize to give OSHA a little more muscle?

A: They do the opposite. A company will protect their workers to the point that they know it is necessary. They don't want to lose people and cause replacement costs, training new staff, lost productivity. But there are certain things that are more insidious. Long-term illnesses — those with latency periods — might not show up on a particular employer's watch. In some gray areas, OSHA helps keep the playing field level — if they would consistently apply the regulation and enforce them. Unfortunately, it doesn't work that way.

B: Part of OSHA's job is to issue new health and safety standards. How is it done on this front?

A: OSHA's standard setting process has become better and better. But many factors are still out of their reach.

B: What's that supposed to mean?

A: Actually, the enterprises also take responsibility for the safety of the workers. The vast majority of work-related fatalities are preventable. If you look at the best and worst countries or the best and worst companies in serious sectors, there's a big difference in the number of accidents at work. That's clear evidence that most of those accidents could be prevented. The culture of a company will have a great influence on the safety production.

Part IV   Reading Material

Classification of Lubrication Oils

Lubricating oils used are tested for a number of properties. These include viscosity, pour point, flash point, fire point, auto-ignition point, demulsibility, neutralization number, and precipitation number. Standard test methods are used for each test. The properties of lube oil are briefly explained in the following paragraphs.

Viscosity

The viscosity of the oil is its tendency to resist flow. A liquid of high viscosity flows very slowly. In variable climates, for example, automobile owners change oil according to prevailing seasons. Oil changes are necessary because heavy oil becomes too thick or sluggish in cold weather, and light oil becomes too thin in hot weather. The higher the temperature of the oil, the lower its viscosity becomes; lowering the temperature increases the viscosity. On a cold morning, it is the high viscosity of stiffness of the lube oil that makes an automobile engine difficult to start. The viscosity must always be high enough to keep a good oil film between the moving parts. Otherwise, friction will increase, resulting in power loss and rapid wear on the parts.

Oils are graded by their viscosities at a certain temperature. Grading is getting up by noting the number of seconds required for a given quantity (60 mL) of the oil at the given temperature to flow through a standard orifice. The right grade of oil, therefore, means oil of the proper viscosity.

Every kind of oil has the viscosity index based on the slope of the temperature-viscosity curve. The viscosity index depends on the rate of change in viscosity of the given oil with a change in temperature. A low index figure means a steep slope of the curve, or a great variation of viscosity with a change in temperature; a high index figure means a flatter slope, or less variation of viscosity with the same changes in temperature. If you are using the oil with a high viscosity index, its viscosity will change less when the temperature of the engine increases.

Pour Point

The pour point of the oil is the lowest temperature at which the oil will barely flow from a container. At a temperature below the pour point, oil congeals of solidifies. Lube oils used in cold weather operations must have a low pour point. (**NOTE**: The pour point is closely related to the viscosity of the oil. In general, an oil of high viscosity will have a higher pour point than an oil of low viscosity.)

Flash Point

The flash point of the oil is the temperature at which enough vapor is given off to flash when a flame or a spark is present. The minimum flash points allowed for navy lube oils are all above 300 °F. However, the temperature of the oils is always far below 300 °F under normal operating conditions.

Fire Point

The fire point of the oil is the temperature at which the oil will continue to burn when it is ignited.

Auto-Ignition Point

The auto-ignition point of the oil is the temperature at which the flammable vapors given off from the oil will burn. This kind of burning will occur without the application of a spark of a flame. For most lubricating oils, this temperature is in the range of 465 °F to 815 °F.

Demulsibility

The demulsibility, or emulsion characteristic, of the oil is its ability to separate cleanly from any water present — an important factor in forced-feed lubrication systems. You should keep water (fresh of salt) out of oils.

Neutralization Number

The neutralization number of the oil indicates its acid content and is defined as the number of milligrams of potassium hydroxide (KOH) required to neutralize 1 gram of the oil. All petroleum products deteriorate (oxidize) in air and heat. Oxidation produces organic acids which, if present in sufficient concentrations, will cause deterioration of alloy bearings at elevated temperature, galvanized surfaces, and demulsibility of the oil with respect to fresh water and salt water. The increase in acidity with use is an index of deterioration and is measured as a part of the work factor test. This test is not applicable to 9,250 oil.

Precipitation Number

The precipitation number of the oil is a measure of the amount of solids classified as asphalts or carbon residue contained in the oil. The number is reached when a known amount of oil is diluted with naphtha and the precipitate is separated by centrifuging — the volume of separated solids equals the precipitation number. This test detects the presence of foreign materials in used oils. The oil with a high precipitation number may cause trouble in an engine. It would leave deposits or plug up valves and pumps.

Unit 11 New Type Automobile Engine

Part I Illustrated English

Diagram of New Power Vehicle

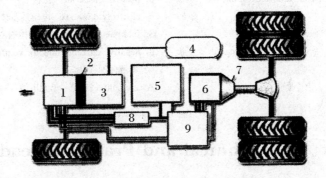

Fig. 11-1 Structure of SHEV (Series Hybrid Electrical Vehicle)
1. alternator 交流发电机
2. overdrive gear 增速齿轮
3. engine 发动机
4. fuel tank 燃料箱
5. battery pack 电池组
6. rectifier 整流器
7. controller 控制器
8. driving system 驱动系统
9. control system 控制系统

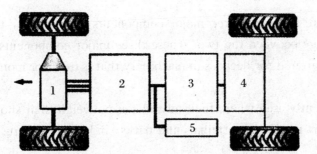

Fig. 11-2 Basic Components of Fuel Cell Electric Vehicle
1. driving system 驱动系统
2. control system 控制系统
3. fuel cell 燃料电池
4. fuel tank 燃料箱
5. battery pack 电池组

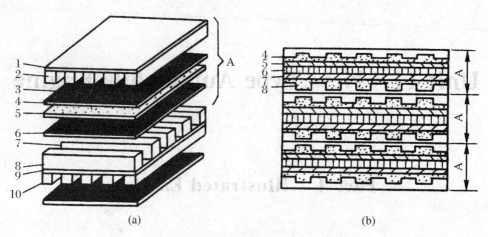

Fig. 11-3 Basic Structure of Fuel Cell

(a) Structure of Fuel Cell Body; (b) Fuel Cell Stack

1. negative current collector reinforcing rib 负极集流体加强肋
2./10. separator 隔离板、集流板
3. positive current collector reinforcing rib 正极集流体加强肋
4./7. air passage 空气通道
5. positive electrode 正极
6. electrolyte matrix 电解质基体
8. fuel gas passage 燃料气体通道
9. negative current collector reinforcing rib 负极集流体加强肋
A. elementary cell 单元电池

Part Ⅱ Technical and Practical Reading

Electric Vehicle

An Electric Vehicle, or EV, is a vehicle driven by an electric motor instead of an Internal Combustion Engine (ICE), and fueled by electricity from a battery instead of a tank of gasoline.

As such, there are only three major components: the motor, the battery, and a controller of energy between the two. These three major components, in their simplest form, have been around for decades in machinery that is used for months on end without rest.

EVs are presently used where their advantages outweigh their shortcomings, such as passenger transport in airport terminals and parks, industrial lift trucks in factories, or golf carts.

An EV for road use, as either an automobile or a delivery van, is most suitable for urban areas where distances are not too long or the payloads are light. Extensive research has been improving the batteries available for EVs, reducing their cost and weight, and increasing the range of vehicles.

To overcome the limitations of batteries, some EVs are hybrids, using a combination of a battery and an ICE. In such a vehicle, the battery supplies high energy for acceleration while a small ICE runs efficiently at a constant speed while moving the vehicle on the highway. Extended range, high performance, reduced pollution and increased efficiency is the outcome.

Most present-day EVs don't look much different from ICE vehicles. They are conversions of existing ICE vehicles. Using an existing vehicle eliminates the problem of designing from scratch, but it sacrifices performance and efficiency due to the heavy weight and poor aerodynamics. However, some electric cars have an unusual appearance for a number of reasons. They may be more aerodynamic to reduce energy consumption. Some use large quantities of non-rusting materials so that the car body can last longer because electric drive trains tend to have very long life spans. Some have unusual shapes to accommodate a large battery pack row within the vehicle to lower the center of gravity, allowing for handling. And some EV makers just want to be sure that you know that this vehicle is something special and worth a second look.

We must use energy wisely, more efficiently, and an EV uses less than half the energy of an ICE. In the city, where 80 to 90 percent of driving occurs, the gasoline engine gets its worst mileage whereas the EV gets its best. The electric motor in an EV is not running when stopped in traffic and therefore consumes no energy. Also, EVs can be equipped with regenerative braking which puts energy back into the batteries while slowing to a stop. Because of the increased efficiency of EVs and the fact that recharging would take place mostly at night, millions of electric vehicles could be put into use in North America with no increase in electrical generating capacity being required. In the most extreme ease, an all-electric car in North America would increase electric power plant demand by only 20% or so.

The ICE automobile is responsible for almost 80% of air pollution in our cities. Air quality is thus the driving force for finding a replacement for the ICE auto. An EV produces no emissions by itself and is responsible for only a small portion of power plant wastes. In Canada, 60% of the electricity is generated by hydro, which causes no air pollution. Furthermore, EVs reduce more air pollution. They reduce water pollution by virtue of reducing the amount of petroleum products being produced, transported, stored, used and disposed of. Every one of these activities contributes to pollution, refinery waste products and emissions, spills from tanker ships and tanker trucks, leaks from storage tanks and vehicle crankcases, and disposal by burning or being dumped into waterways and sewage systems. EVs are quieter than Otto and Diesel cycle engines, so they reduce the level of noise pollution. EVs produce far less waste heat than combustion engines (also known as heat engines), so they reduce the amount of heat pollution being produced.

At today's gasoline price, an EVs fuel cost is much less. Battery replacement costs over the life of the car are less than the costs of ICE tune-ups. The purchase price of an EV is presently higher than a comparable car, but total lifetime costs are about equal.

Continuing research and mass production will lower both electric vehicle and battery costs in the future.

Present day EVs can satisfy most requirements in city driving. The range of EVs can be from 50 km to 200 km, top speeds vary from 50 km/hr to 140 km/hr, and the acceleration is from sedate to outperforming sports cars.

California has backed down on its 1998 deadline by which it required auto makers to have 2% of the vehicles they sold are zero-emission vehicles. Since the only zero-emission vehicle is the EV, the state was essentially mandating EVs. Similar legislation with the 1998 deadline is still in place in Massachusetts and the state of New York. In California, the requirement for 10% of vehicle sales to be zero-emission vehicles by 2003 is still in force.

American and Japanese auto makers are both working to meet these requirements. The U.S. government will have spent over $300 million by 1998 on EV and battery research and development programs.

New Words

1. fuel [fjuəl] vt. 供给燃料
2. outweigh [aʊt'weɪ] v. 在重量（或价值等）上超过
3. shortcoming ['ʃɔːrtkʌmɪŋ] n. 短处，缺点
4. terminal ['tɜːrmɪnl] adj. 末端的；终端，终点站
5. payload ['peɪloʊd] n. （运输工具的）净载重量
6. extensive [ɪk'stɛnsɪv] adj. 广博的，广泛的
7. gradually ['grædʒuəli] adv. 逐渐地，逐步地
8. hybrid ['haɪbrɪd] n. [动、植]杂种；混合物
9. conversion [kən'vɜːrʒn] n. 转变，更新
10. sacrifice ['sækrəˌfaɪs] v. 牺牲
11. aerodynamics [ˌeroʊdaɪ'næmɪks] n. 空气动力学
12. rust [rʌst] n./v. 锈；生锈
13. last [læst] vi. 持续，支持，维持
14. gravity ['grævɪti] n. 地心引力，重力
15. wisely ['waɪzli] adv. 聪明地，精明地
16. mileage ['maɪlɪdʒ] n. 里程
17. recharge [riː'tʃɑːdʒ] v. 再充电
18. replacement [rɪ'pleɪsmənt] n. 代替，替换
19. refinery [rɪ'faɪnəri] n. 精炼厂
20. spill [spɪl] v. 漏出，溢出，漏失
21. disposal [dɪ'spoʊzl] n. 处置，对付
22. dump [dʌmp] v. 倾倒，倾卸
23. waterway ['wɔːtərweɪ] n. 水路，排水沟
24. sewage ['suɪdʒ] n. 下水道系统
25. tune-up ['tjuːnˌʌp] n. 发动机的调整
26. lifetime ['laɪfˌtaɪm] n. 一生，终生，寿命
27. mass [mæs] adj. 大规模的，集中的
28. sedate [sɪ'det] adj. 安静的，镇静的
29. outperform [ˌaʊtpər'fɔːrm] v. 胜过
30. deadline ['dɛdˌlaɪn] n. 期限，有效期

31. zero ['zɪroʊ] n. 零,零位,零点
32. mandate ['mæn,det] n./v. 命令,指令;批准
33. essentially [ɪ'senʃəli] adv. 实质上,本来

Phrases and Expressions

1. EV 电动汽车
2. electric motor car 电动机车,电瓶车
3. ICE (Internal Combustion Engine) 内燃机
4. as much 同样地,同量地
5. on end 连续地
6. passenger transport 旅客运输
7. airport terminal （城市里的）航空集散站
8. lift truck 叉车
9. golf cart 高尔夫球器械装运车
10. delivery van 厢式送货车
11. design from scratch 从头设计
12. life span 寿命
13. electric drive trains 电力驱动系
14. battery pack 蓄电池组
15. the center of gravity 重心
16. regenerative braking 再生制动,能量回收式制动
17. put into use 使用
18. electric power plant 电力驱动装置,电力装置,发电厂
19. by virtue of 依靠,由于
20. back down 放弃原主张,让步
21. in force 有效地

Notes to Text

1. EVs can be equipped with regenerative braking which puts energy back into the batteries while slowing to a stop.
电动汽车配有再生制动能量的回收装置,它可把车制动时的能量回收到蓄电池。

2. EVs are quieter than Otto and Diesel cycle of engines, so they reduce the level of noise pollution.
电动汽车工作起来比汽油机和柴油机安静,因此它减少了噪音污染。

3. We must use energy wisely, more efficiently, and an EV uses less than half the energy of an ICE.
我们必须明智、有效地利用能源,一辆电动汽车使用的能源不到内燃机的一半。

4. In the city, where 80 to 90 percent of driving occurs, the gasoline engine gets its worse mileage whereas the EV gets its best.
在城市里,80%到90%的车辆行驶时,汽油发动机都会随着行驶里程的增加而工况下降,而电动汽车则不会。

5. Air quality is thus the driving force for finding a replacement for the ICE auto.
提高空气质量是寻找内燃机汽车代替品的动力。

Exercises

1. **Answer the following questions to the text.**

(1) What is an electric vehicle?
(2) How many major components are there in an EV? What are they?
(3) Why do some electric cars have an unusual appearance?
(4) Why can an EV use energy more efficiently than an ICE?
(5) Why do EVs reduce air pollution?

2. **Translate the following phrases and expressions into Chinese.**

(1) battery pack
(2) electric power plant
(3) regenerative braking
(4) delivery van
(5) ICE
(6) lift truck

3. **Translate the following sentences into Chinese.**

(1) The advantages of using an existing vehicle are that it eliminates the problem of designing from scratch, but it sacrifices performance and efficiency due to the heavy weight and poor aerodynamics.

(2) The ICE automobile is responsible for almost 80% of the air pollution in our cities.

(3) Battery replacement costs over the life of the car are less than the costs of ICE tune-ups.

(4) In California, the requirement for 10% of vehicle sales to be zero-emission vehicles by 2003 is still in force.

(5) The U. S. government will have spent over $300 million by 1998 on EV and battery research and development programs.

(6) The purchase price of an EV is presently higher than a comparable car, but total lifetime costs are about equal.

Part Ⅲ Listening and Speaking

New Technologies A

A—Paul B—Jack

A: Although automobile was invented over 100 years ago, substantial technical advances have still been achieved in automobile during the last decade.

B: That's true. The technical advances have been made particularly in such automotive areas as the closed-loop controlled catalyst, the four-valve technology, the four-wheel drive and steering, etc.

A: Since so many advances have been achieved in automotive technology, I don't know whether it is possible to have any further improvements in future automobile.

B: Certainly. The automobile will surely be further developed in future. You know the development of automobile, especially in the last 40 years, shows that technical advances can make it possible to improve all the significant qualities of an automobile like space, comfort, reliability, performance, fuel economy, and safety. And ...

A: I'm sorry to interrupt you, but I don't know much about the automotive development in the last 40 years. Can you tell me something about it, please?

B: OK. In the last 40 years, automobile has been developed greatly. For instance, the 1950's witnessed the broad introduction of automatic transmissions and electric servo actuators. The automotive development at the end of the 1960's and the beginning of the 1970's was marked by the stiffening of exhaust-gas regulations in the United States and other western countries.

A: How about the 1970's and 1980's?

B: During the 1970's, the fuel consumption of automobiles became the focus of worldwide research, but from the middle of the 1980's, a trend to high-output engines began. This trend is still predominant today as signified by the appearance of the four-valve technique, supercharger, and six- to twelve-cylinder engine.

A: Oh, I see. The automotive development tells us that although many technical advances have been achieved, it can still be safely said that the automobile as a means of transportation still has a long developmental potential.

B: That's right. As far as I know, the future automotive development, including design and manufacturing, will be largely influenced by three factors.

A: Only by three factors? What do you mean by the three factors?

B: By the three factors, I mean the technical advances in electronics, materials and computer.

A: Oh, really? Are they very important?

B: Yes, of course. First, electronics have played an essential role in almost all technical solutions. It can be said that only electronics can make a step forward from a mere governing action to closed-loop control. Second, progress in automotive engineering has always been closely tied to progress in material science. The use of new lightweight materials can improve road performance and reduce fuel consumption.

A: Computer must be the third important new technology in automobile design and manufacturing. Right?

B: Yes. Computer is, of course, the important new technology used for further improvements in automotive engineering, design, measurement and test techniques, etc.

A: Now I understand that these three factors will play a decisive role in the future development of automobiles.

New Technologies B

A—Peter   B—Tom

A: Hello, Tom, where did you go yesterday?
B: I went to Beijing International Automotive Exhibition.
A: Really? Was it the one held in New China International Exhibition Center? I heard that it was one of the biggest exhibitions in China.
B: Yes, it's the one. The automotive enterprises from all over the world showed their new models which would be rolled out next year.
A: That sounds amazing. What impressed you the most?
B: Actually, there was a type of conceptual car that caught my eyes. That was biofuel car.
A: Biofuel car? Could you be a bit more precise?
B: It was a car that burns biofuels. The car in that exhibition gets energy from algae-based fuel.
A: Why do we need this kind of car?
B: It's eco-friendly. Coming up with renewable sources of transportation, fuel can wean us from oil. Recent years, researchers are devising ways to turn lumber and crop wastes, garbage and inedible perennials like switchgrass into competitively priced fuels. But the most promising next-generation biofuel comes from algae.
A: Is it truly that significant?
B: Yes. Algae grow fast, consume carbon dioxide and can generate more than 5,000 gallons a year per acre of biofuel. Algae-based fuel can be added directly into existing refining and distribution system; in theory, the U.S. could produce enough of it to meet all of the nation's transportation needs.
A: That's good if it really works out.

Part Ⅳ   Reading Material

Hybrid Electric Vehicle

Hybrid Electric Vehicles (HEVs) are offered by numerous auto manufacturers and are becoming increasingly more available. Today, most people have heard of HEVs and many people have a basic understanding of how they work. Hybrid Electric Vehicles combine the internal combustion engine of a conventional vehicle with the battery and electric motor of an electric vehicle. The combination offers low emissions, with the power, range, and convenient fueling of conventional (gasoline and diesel) vehicles, and they never need to be plugged in. The inherent flexibility of HEVs makes them well suited for fleet and personal transportation.

A Hybrid Electric Vehicle is an optimized mix of various components. It mainly contains the following parts: electric motor, battery, engine, fuel tank, etc.

Electric Motor

The electric motor on a hybrid car is very sophisticated. Advanced electronics allow it to act as a motor as well as a generator. For example, when it needs to, it can draw energy from the batteries to accelerate the car. But acting as a generator, it can slow the car down and return energy to the batteries.

In a HEV, an electric traction motor converts electrical energy from the energy storage unit into mechanical energy that drives the wheels of the vehicle. Unlike a traditional vehicle, where the engine must "ramp up" before full torque can be provided, an electric motor provide full torque at low speed. This characteristic gives the vehicle excellent "off the line" acceleration.

Important characteristics of a HEV motor include good drive control and fault tolerance, as well as low noise and high efficiency. Other characteristics include flexibility in relation to voltage fluctuations and, of course, acceptable mass production costs. Front-running motor technologies for HEV applications include permanent magnet, AC induction, and switched reluctance motors.

Battery

The battery is an essential component of a HEV. Although a few HEVs with advanced batteries have been introduced in the market, no current battery technology has demonstrated an economically acceptable combination of power, energy efficiency, and life cycle for high-volume production vehicles.

Desirable attributes of high-power batteries for HEV applications are high-peak and pulse-specific power, high specific energy at pulse power, a high charge acceptance to maximize regenerative braking utilization, and long calendar and life cycle. Developing methods/designs to balance the packs electrically and thermally, developing accurate techniques to determine a battery's state of charge, developing abuse-tolerant batteries, and recycle are additional technical challenges.

Engine

The hybrid car has an ICE much like the one you will find on most cars. However, the engine on a hybrid is smaller and uses advanced technologies to reduce emissions and increase efficiency.

Fuel Tank

The fuel tank in a hybrid car is the energy storage device for the gasoline engine. Gasoline has a much higher energy density than batteries do. For example, it takes about 1,000 pounds of batteries to store as much energy as 1 gallon (7 pounds) of gasoline.

Transmission

The transmission on a hybrid car performs the same basic function as the transmission on a conventional car. Some hybrids, like the Honda Insight have conventional transmissions. Others, like the Toyota Prius, have radically different ones.

Tomorrow's HEVs will contain a mix of aluminum, steel, plastic, magnesium, and composites (typically a strong, lightweight material composed of fibers in a binding matrix, such as fiberglass). To make these materials affordable and durable, research is intensifying on vehicle manufacturing methods, structural concepts, design analysis tools, sheet-manufacturing processes improved material strength, and recycle. Since 1975, the weight of a typical family sedan has decreased from 4,000 pounds to 3,300 pounds. Researchers are working to reduce overall vehicle weight by yet another 40% to 2,000 pounds. To achieve this, they must reduce the mass of both the outer body and chassis by half, trim power train weight by 10%, and reduce the weight of interior components.

A Hybrid Electric Vehicle has two or more sources of onboard power. The integration of these power-producing components with the electrical energy storage components allows for many different types of HEV designs. A power control strategy is needed to control the flow of power and to maintain adequate reserves of energy in the storage devices. Although this is an added complexity not found in conventional vehicles, it allows the components to work together in an optimal manner to achieve multiple design objectives, such as high fuel economy and low emissions.

The biggest distinction between different hybrid designs is whether they are parallel or series, or a combination of the two. In a parallel design, the Auxiliary Power Unit (APU) can mechanically drive the wheels; in a series design, the APU generates electricity and doesn't directly drive the wheels. A third type combines the best aspects of both, and is sometimes called a combined or a series/parallel design. A combined design allows the APU to directly drive the wheels but also has the ability to charge the energy storage device through a generator. The combined hybrid is a subset of the parallel design since it can directly drive the wheels from the APU. The way the hardware components are connected (parallel, series, or a combination of the two) will be referred to here as the "hardware configuration" and the management of the power flow among the components will be referred to as the "control strategy" or more generally "energy management".

A secondary distinction between hybrids is charge-sustaining versus charge-depleting hardware configurations and control strategies. Charge-depleting vehicles allow their batteries to become depleted and cannot recharge them at the same rate they are being discharged. The common "range-extender" is a charge-depleting vehicle unless the APU is larger than the average power load of the vehicle over a given cycle. A charge-sustaining hybrid has an APU that is adequately sized to meet the average power load, and if operated under the expected conditions, will be able to keep adequate electrical energy storage reserves indefinitely.

Hybrid Electric Vehicles are powered by two energy sources—an energy conversion unit (such as a combustion engine or fuel cell) and an energy storage device (such as batteries or ultra capacitors). The energy conversion unit may be powered by gasoline, methanol, compressed natural gas, hydrogen, or other alternative fuels. Hybrid electric vehicles have the potential to be two to three times more fuel-efficient than conventional vehicles.

When the vehicle is started, the gasoline engine "warms up". If necessary, the electric motor acts as a generator, converting energy from the engine into electricity and storing it in the battery.

The gasoline engine powers the vehicle at cruising speed and, if needed, provides power to the battery for later use.

During heavy accelerating or when additional power is needed, the gasoline engine and electric motor are both used to propel the vehicle. Additional power from the battery is used to power the electric motor as needed.

Regenerative braking converts otherwise wasted energy from braking into electricity and stores it in the battery. In regenerative braking, the electric motor is reversed so that, instead of using electricity to turn the wheels, the rotating wheels turn the motor and create electricity using energy from the wheels to slow the vehicle down.

If additional stopping power is needed, conventional friction brakes (e.g., disc brakes) are also applied automatically. When the vehicle is stopped, such as a red light, the gasoline engine and electric motor are shut off automatically, so that energy is not wasted at idling. The battery continues to power auxiliary systems, such as the air conditioning and dashboard displays.

Hybrids should be competitively priced when all the costs over the life of the vehicle are included. This is because any cost premium is likely to be offset by fuel savings. A federal tax deduction of $2000 for the purchase of a hybrid vehicle is available in many cases, and some states may provide additional incentives to encourage the purchase of hybrid vehicles.

There are three hybrid cars on the market today: the two-seater Honda Insight, the five-seater Toyota Prius and the five-seater Honda Civic. Other major automakers have announced their intentions to introduce hybrids within the next few years.

Unit 12 Manual Transmissions

Part Ⅰ Illustrated English

Diagram of Manual Transmissions Structure

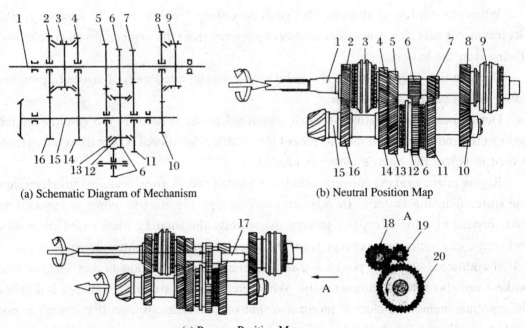

(a) Schematic Diagram of Mechanism

(b) Neutral Position Map

(c) Reverse Position Map

Fig. 12-1 Schematic Diagram of Santana 2000GSi 330 Type Transmission Mechanism

1. primary shaft　第一轴
2. primary shaft 4 block gear　第一轴 4 挡齿轮
3. 3,4 block synchronization device joint sleeve　3、4 挡同步器接合套
4. primary shaft 3 block gear　第一轴 3 挡齿轮
5. primary shaft 2 block gear　第一轴 2 挡齿轮
6. backward gear　倒挡齿轮
7. primary shaft 1 block gear　第一轴 1 挡齿轮
8. primary shaft 5 block gear　第一轴 5 挡齿轮
9. 5 block synchronization device joint sleeve assembly　5 挡接合套同步器组件
10. main shaft 5 block gear　第二轴 5 挡齿轮
11. main shaft 1 block gear　第二轴 1 挡齿轮
12. 1,2 block synchronization device joint sleeve assembly　1,2 挡接合套同步器组件
13. main shaft 2 block gear　第二轴 2 挡齿轮
14. main shaft 3 block gear　第二轴 3 挡齿轮
15. main shaft　第二轴
16. main shaft 4 block gear　第二轴 4 挡齿轮
17. reversing shaft　倒挡轴
18. reversing shaft gear　倒挡轴齿轮
19. primary shaft backward gear　第一轴倒挡齿轮
20. main shaft backward gear　第二轴倒挡齿轮

Part Ⅱ Technical and Practical Reading

Manual Transmissions

Torque that is produced at the end of the crankshaft by the engine must be transmitted to the driving wheels. To accomplish this, torque must first pass through the clutch and transmission.

The purpose of a transmission is to apply different torque forces to the driving wheels. Vehicles are required to perform under many types of loads. Stopping and starting, heavy loads, high speeds, and small loads are examples of the different demands placed on the vehicle. The transmission is designed to change the torque applied to the driving wheels for different applications. In addition, the transmission is used to reverse the vehicle direction and to provide neutral (no power) to the wheels. Normally, less torque is needed with higher speeds and smaller loads. When slower speeds and higher loads are used, more torque is needed.

The transmission is a case of gears located behind the clutch. The output of the clutch drives the set of gears. The case that houses the gears is attached to the clutch housing. There are several shafts with different-sized gears inside the case. As the gears are shifted to different ratios, different torques can be selected for different operational conditions. Although there are many parts in the transmission, the main ones include the drive, or input gear, the counter shaft gear (also called the cluster gear) with four gears on it, the main shaft with two gears on it, and the reverse idler gear. The counter shaft gears all turn at the same speed. The low and reverse gear and the second and high-speed are able to slide on the main shaft spline.

Vehicle designs have been changing over the past several years. Several types of transmissions have been developed, including four-speed, five-speed, and transaxle transmission.

The four-speed manual transmission has an additional gear set to produce four forward gears. With four gears, a wider range of torque characteristics is available. Increased torque range is usually needed for smaller engines.

Five-speed transmissions are used on many vehicles today. With five gears, the range of torque is increased so that a smaller engine can be used.

The transaxle system is used on front-wheel drive vehicles that have the transmission and final drive gearing placed together. Many designs are used for transaxles. The principles are much the same as any manual transmission.

During normal shifting patterns, gears must be engaged and disengaged. Most gears, however, are not turning at the same speed before being engaged. To eliminate gears clashing with each other during normal downshifting or upshifting, synchronizers are used. Synchronizers are used in all forward speeds in today's manual transmissions. There are several types of synchronizers, but they all work on a similar principle. If the gear speeds can be synchronized or put at the same speed, they will mesh easily and there will be little clash or clatter. The assembly is made of an input gear, several cone surfaces, a ring gear sliding sleeve, the hub, several spring-loaded steel balls, and the internal gear.

The transmission case is used to hold the gears for proper shifting. The case is bolted to the clutch housing with several bolts. It is made of aluminum or cast iron for strength and support. The transmission case also includes an extension housing that contains the transmission output shaft.

Many transmissions use gear oil for lubrication. Gear oil is a type of lubrication used to keep gears well lubricated. Each manufacturer typically recommends its own type of gear oil.

The gears on a manual transmission must be moved or shifted to engage different gears. Shifting forks of arms are used to move the synchronizers back and forth to engage the gears. There are several types of shifting forks.

As the operator moves the shift linkage, the fork moves the synchronizer for a specific gear.

Detent springs, balls, and rollers are used to hold the shifting fork in the correct gear position to ensure full engagement.

There are many designs of shifting mechanisms. Certain vehicles have the shift lever on the steering wheel column, while others have a floor shift system. Both mechanical linkages and cables can be used to transfer the shift lever movement to the shifting forks.

New Words

1. transmission [træns'mɪʃən, trænz-] n. 变速器
2. manual ['mænjuəl] adj. 用手的；手制的，手工的
3. torque [tɔːrk] n. 扭转力；转（力）矩
4. crankshaft ['kræŋkʃæft] adj. 机轴；曲轴
5. clutch [klʌtʃ] n. 紧抓；控制；离合器
6. neutral ['nuːtrəl] n. 空挡位置
7. transaxle [træns'æksl] n. 驱动桥
8. gearing ['ɡɪrɪŋ] n. 传动装置
9. disengaged [ˌdɪsɪn'ɡedʒd] adj. 脱离的
10. downshift ['daʊnˌʃɪft] n. 换低速挡
11. upshift ['ʌpˌʃɪft] n. 换高速挡
12. synchronizer ['sɪŋkrənaɪzə] n. 同步器
13. clatter ['klætɚ] v. 发出咔哒声
14. hub [hʌb] n. 轮轴
15. bolt [boʊlt] n. 螺栓，螺钉
16. lubrication [ˌlubrɪ'keʃən] n. 润滑，加油；润滑作用

Phrases and Expressions

1. manual transmissions 手动变速器
2. driving wheels 驱动轮
3. in addition 另外；除此之外；并且；况且
4. clutch housing 离合器壳
5. input gear 输入齿轮
6. counter shaft gear 副轴齿轮
7. transaxle transmission 变速传动
8. cone surfaces 锥表面
9. a ring gear sliding sleeve 环形齿轮滑动套筒
10. spring-loaded steel ball 弹簧钢球
11. output shaft 输出轴；从动轴
12. gear oil 齿轮油
13. shifting forks 换挡叉
14. shift linkage 换挡连杆
15. shift lever 变速杆

Notes to Text

1. Torque that is produced at the end of the crankshaft by the engine must be transmitted to the driving wheels.

发动机产生的在曲轴的末端的转矩必须传给驱动轮。

2. To accomplish this, torque must first pass through the clutch and transmission.

要做到这一点，扭矩必须先通过离合器和变速器。

3. In addition, the transmission is used to reverse the vehicle direction and to provide neutral (no power) to the wheels.

此外，变速器是用来扭转车辆方向的，并为车轮提供空挡（无动力）的。

4. The transaxle system is used on front-wheel drive vehicles that have the transmission and final drive gearing placed together.

驱动桥系统用于前轮驱动的车辆，变速器和最终传动装置放在一起。

5. Many transmissions use gear oil for lubrication. Gear oil is a type of lubrication used to keep gears well lubricated.

许多变速器都使用齿轮油润滑。齿轮油是一种用于保持齿轮润滑的润滑方式。

Exercises

1. Answer the following questions to the text.

  (1) What is the purpose of a transmission?
  (2) Where is the transmission placed?
  (3) Which types of transmissions have been developed?
  (4) What is the role of transmission case?
  (5) How the transmission to be lubricated?

2. Translate the following phrases and expressions into Chinese.

  (1) primary shaft

(2) backward gear

(3) clutch housing

(4) transaxle transmission

(5) shifting fork

(6) shift linkage

3. Translate the following sentences into Chinese.

(1) The purpose of a transmission is to apply different torque forces to the driving wheels.

(2) The transmission is designed to change the torque applied to the driving wheels for different applications.

(3) Battery replacement costs over the life of the car are less than the costs of ICE tune-ups.

(4) Five-speed transmissions are used on many vehicles today.

(5) Gear oil is a type of lubrication used to keep gears well lubricated.

(6) The gears on a manual transmission must be moved or shifted to engage different gears.

Part Ⅲ   Listening and Speaking

Introduction of New Models A

A—Salesperson   B—Mr. Smith

A: This way, Mr. Smith. What do you think about our new model Audi A6 Quattro?

B: Oh, it looks good. But I'd like to know something about its feature.

A: It's auto transmission and 4-wheel drive with power brakes. Let me tell you more specifications. The engine is 4.2 liter V6. The price is $27,299. I think it's quite a good car.

B: Yes, I think so. But I'd like to look around and make a decision after seeing some other models.

A: Sure. What about this 2000 Toyota Land cruiser?

B: Oh, it looks nice.

A: Yes, I bet you'll like it more after my introduction. It's Power Steering with Alloy Wheels, Cruise Control 4-Wheel Drive.

B: Very good. Could you tell me more about the specifications of this model?

A: Sure. As you can see, it's of sports utility body style with mahogany exterior and 4.7 liter V8 engine and it has excellent safety features, like dual air bags and ABS brakes.

B: What are ABS brakes?

A: Anti-lock braking system, it keeps you from skidding on the road and the newer cars have them.
B: Okay. That's great. What's the price?
A: $49,975.
B: Any discount?
A: Yes, We can offer you 5% off.
B: Good. I'll take it.

Introduction of New Models B

A—Customer   B—Salesperson

A: I like the Honda Accord you showed me before. I think it's more practical for my needs.
B: Alright, sir. You are making a good choice. Honda has made a lot of design improvements in the new Accord.
A: What does it come with standard?
B: On all our new cars, the standards include air conditioning, anti-lock brakes, air bags, and an AM/FM stereo with a CD player. But on the Accord, there is another standard item as well. The Accord comes with cruise control.
A: Cruise control? I don't like that.
B: Why not, sir?
A: I think it's dangerous. What if I can't turn it off?
B: Well, sir, I know some of our customers are concerned about cruise control. But Honda has never had a single cruise control malfunction that led to an accident.
A: I wish it didn't have cruise control. My wife doesn't like it either.
B: You know, sir, you don't have to use it. You can turn it on or off. If you don't want to use it, you just never turn it on.
A: I suppose. And what about the sunroof? Is that standard?
B: No, the sunroof is optional, sir.
A: I see. Another important question is the time I can get this car. I need a new car rather soon.
B: Well, I can say that the new models will be here in August. If you order one now, we will have it for you in August.
A: That's good enough, I think. What colors does the new Accord come in?
B: We have this new model in red, white, black, or silver. These are the standard colors. Of course you could specially order from various other colors too.
A: My brother has last year's Accord. And his car is a kind of soft purple color mixed with silver. I really like that color. I wonder if I can get that color on my Accord.
B: I know the color you mean. Is this it, sir?
A: Yes, I think that's it. Can I get that on the Accord?

B: Yes, you can. That color is very popular with Honda buyers. So we've kept it available.

A: Well, I think I want to order the new Accord then. It looks like an excellent car.

B: You have made a good choice, sir. I drive an Accord myself. They are very solidly built machines, very reliable.

A: Yes, I know. I think Honda is the most reliable car on the road. I would never change to anything else. The Honda I have now almost never has service problems. It runs smooth as silk.

B: Alright, sir. I will get the paperwork ready for you. Just a moment.

Part Ⅳ Reading Material

Dual Clutch Transmission

Unlike the general automatic transmission system, Dual Clutch Transmission (DCT) is based on manual transmission device instead of automatic transmission. In addition to having the flexibility of a manual transmission and the comfort of an automatic transmission, DCT also can provide uninterrupted output power. The conventional manual transmission use only one clutch, the driver must step down the clutch pedal when shift so that the different gears could mesh, and power is discontinuous during shift intermittent which makes the output interrupted.

Differences Between the Two

There are wet dual clutch transmission and dry dual clutch transmission. There is no essential difference between dry dual clutch transmission and wet clutch transmission from the working principle and basic structure, the difference is that the cooling mode of the double clutch friction plate. Two sets clutch disc of the wet clutch are in a sealed oil tank, which absorbs heat by transmission oil soaking the clutch disc, but the dry clutch friction plate doesn't have the sealed oil tank, it cools down by the air.

In 1940, a professor in Darmstadt University, Rudolph Franke, first applied for a patent for a dual clutch transmission that had been tested on a truck, but had not been put into mass production. Subsequently, Porsche also invented the dual clutch transmission specially used in the racecar. However, it failed to put DCT/PDK technology into mass production in that era.

In 1985, Audi applied the dual clutch technology to the racecar field, which was named Sport Quattro S1 Audi racecar with the dual clutch technology. Double clutch technology made Audi race car gallope the off road racing and win a number of the games.

By the end of 1990s, Volkswagen and Berg Warner worked together to produce the first Dual Tronic (R) technology for mass production and application in the mainstream models of dual clutch transmission.

By using the new electronic hydraulic components, the Borg Warner Corporation has turned DCT into a highly practical transmission.

In 2002, DCT was applicated in Germany Volkswagen Golf R32 and Audi V6 TT.

In 2003, it had been extended to other models, such as golf.

In 2004, DCT in Germany Volkswagen Touran (Touran) models matched with the TDI diesel engine for the first time.

Berg Warner's new DCT project was put into operation in 2007, and was mainly for luxury passenger cars, sports cars. The annual production capacity was of 600 thousand sets.

Technology Application

In November 2007, when Berg Warner announced the full implementation of the plan, it was expected to face 2.3 million dual clutch transmissions with its innovative Dual Tronic Technology (R) every year.

This significant growth was driven by the first listing of the company's dual clutch transmission technology. The technology won the business from transmission and vehicle manufacturers all over the world including projects with VW, Audi, Bugatti, Shanghai Automotive Industry Corporation and Nissan (nsany) project and Getrag (Getrag) and five global auto makers.

There are many companies of which the transmission is based on DCT technology, including Volkswagen DSG (Direct Shift Gearbox), Audi S Tronic, BMW M DKG (Doppel Kuppling Getriebe, M Double Clutch gearbox), Ford, Volvo PowerShift, Porsche PDK (Porsche Doppel Kupplung), Mitsubishi TC-SST (Twin Clutch-Super Sport Transmission), Nissan GR6 (Rear Gearbox 6 Speed) and BYD DCT (Dual clutch transmission).

Core Technology

What is the core technology of the dual clutch transmission? Many people think that it must be double clutch. Actually it's not. Dual clutch is just the most important features of this type of clutch, and its key technical characteristics are more than this one.

Power out of the engine is output from a shaft, and it also needs the input power from one shaft to drive the wheels. But the most fundamental purpose of the dual clutch is to use its two clutches with one working and the other preparing to transfer power in two ways. The designers devise hollow shaft cleverly, which means there is a shaft inside, which is a tube and then set a shaft. It can transmit power in part time.

This design solves the contradiction between power transmission and the space occupied cleverly. Although ingenious, it requires higher accuracy in the real manufacturing process, which may be the reason that it has been more than 40 years before they are put into production after the technology was invented.

The core technology of DCT is mastered in the United States Berg Wanner (BorgWarner) and Germany (Schaeffler) group. Berg Warner is the provider of the key technology for Volkswagen's first generation six speed DSG (public DCT), and provides a wet dual clutch mass DSG for Volkswagen. In the spring of 2009, Volkswagen released a new generation of dry seven speed dual clutch transmission, provided by the Luk Company under the flag of the German Schaeffler Group. The domestic automobile manufacturers BYD also masters the most important dual clutch module technology in dual clutch gearbox in 2011 and the fully independent design ability of dual clutch electronic control system, with its turbocharged cylinder direct injection engine columns packed in the new production G6 and speed sharp models, narrowing the gap between domestic and world's advanced car prices in the power train.

Unit 13 Automatic Transmissions

Part I Illustrated English

Diagram of Automatic Transmissions

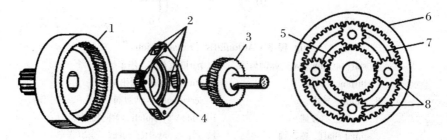

Fig. 13-1 The Simple Planetary Gear System

1./6. ring gear 齿圈   3./5. sun gear 太阳轮
2./8. planet gear 行星轮   4./7. planet carrier 行星架

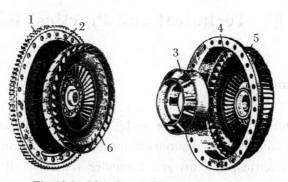

Fig. 13-2 Main Parts of Torque Converters

1. start up ring gear 起动齿圈   4. impeller 泵轮
2./5. converter 变矩器壳   6. turbine 涡轮
3. stator 导轮

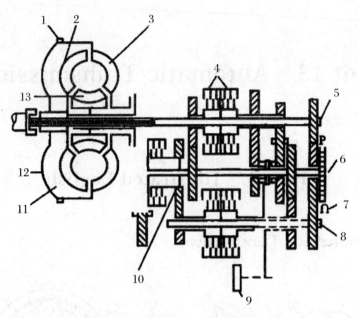

Fig. 13-3 Automatic Transmission
1. start up ring gear 起动齿圈
2. turbine 涡轮
3. stator 导轮
4. clutch 离合器
5. input shaft 输入轴
6. countershaft 中间轴
7. parking lock 停车锁
8. output shaft 输出轴
9. servo value 伺服阀
10. one-way clutch 单向离合器
11./12. converter cover 变矩器壳
13. impeller 泵轮

Part Ⅱ Technical and Practical Reading

Automatic Transmissions

The modern automatic transmission is by far the most complicated mechanical component in today's automobile. Automatic transmissions contain mechanical systems, hydraulic systems, electrical systems and computer controls, all working together in perfect harmony which goes virtually unnoticed until there is a problem. This article will help you understand the concepts behind what goes on inside these technological marvels and what goes into repairing them when they fail.

What Is a Transmission?

The transmission is a device that is connected to the back of the engine and sends the power from the engine to the drive wheels. An automobile engine runs at best at a certain RPM (revolutions per minute) range and it is the transmission's job to make sure that the power is delivered to the wheels while keeping the engine within that range. It does this through various gear combinations. In first gear, the engine turns much faster in relation to the drive wheels, while in high gear the engine is loafing even though the car may be going in excess of 70 MPH (miles per hour). In addition to the various forward gears, a transmission also has a neutral position which disconnects the engine from the drive wheels, and reverse, which causes the drive wheels to turn in the opposite direction allowing you to back up. Finally, there is the park position. In this position, a latch mechanism (not unlike a deadbolt lock on a door) is inserted into a slot in the output shaft to lock the drive wheels and keep them from turning, thereby preventing the vehicle from rolling.

There are two basic types of automatic transmissions based on whether the vehicle is rear wheel drive or front wheel drive.

On a rear wheel drive car, the transmission is usually mounted to the back of the engine and is located under the hump in the center of the floorboard alongside the gas pedal position. A drive shaft connects the rear of the transmission to the final drive which is located in the rear axle and is used to send power to the rear wheels. Power flow on this system is simple and straight forward going from the engine, through the torque converter, then through the transmission and drive shaft until it reaches the final drive where it is split and sent to the two rear wheels.

On a front wheel drive car, the transmission is usually combined with the final drive to form what is called a transaxle. The engine on a front wheel drive car is usually mounted sideways in the car with the transaxle tucked under it on the side of the engine facing the rear of the car.

Front axles are connected directly to the transaxle and provide power to the front wheels. In this example, power flows from the engine, through the torque converter to a large chain that sends the power through a 180 degree turn to the transmission that is alongside the engine. From there, the power is routed through the transmission to the final drive where it is split and sent to the two front wheels through the drive axles.

There are a number of other arrangements including front drive vehicles where the engine is mounted front to back instead of sideways and there are other systems that drive all four wheels. But the two systems described here are by far the most popular. A much less popular rear drive arrangement has the transmission mounted directly to the final drive at the rear and is connected by a drive shaft to the torque converter which is still mounted on the engine. This system is found on the new corvette and is used in order to balance the weight evenly between the front and the rear wheels for improved performance and handing. Another rear drive system mounts everything: the engine, the transmission and the final drive in the rear engine arrangement is popular on the Porsche.

Transmission Components

The modern automatic transmission consists of many components and systems that are designed to work together in a symphony of clever mechanical, hydraulic and electrical technology that has evolved over the years into what many mechanically inclined individuals consider to be an art form. We try to use simple, generic explanations, which is possible to describe these systems but, due to the complexity of some of these components, you may have to use some mental gymnastics to visualize their operation.

The main components of an automatic transmission are as follows:

Planetary gear sets which are the mechanical systems that provide the various forward gear rations as well as reverse.

The hydraulic system which uses a special transmission fluid sent under pressure by an oil pump through the valve body to control the clutches and the bands in order to control the planetary gear out.

Seals and gaskets are used to keep the oil where it is supposed to be and prevent it from leaking out.

The torque converter acts like a clutch to allow the vehicle to come to a stop in gear while the engine is still running.

The governor and the modulator or throttle cable monitor speed and throttle position in order to determine when to shift.

On newer vehicles, shift points are controlled by computer which direct selectrical solenoids to shift oil flow to the appropriate component at the right instant.

Planetary Gear Sets

Automatic transmissions contain many gears in various combinations. In a manual Transmission, gears slide along shafts as you move the shift lever from one position to another, engaging various sized gears as required in order to provide the correct gear ratio. In an automatic transmission, however, the gears are never physically moved and are always engaged to the same gears. This is accomplished through the use of planetary gear sets.

The basic planetary gear sets consist of a sun gear, a ring gear and two or more planet gears, all remaining in constant mesh, a common carrier which allows the gears to spin on shafts called "pinions" which are attached to the carrier.

One example of a way that this system can be used is by connecting the ring gear to the input shaft coming from the engine, connecting the planet carrier to the output shaft, and locking the sun gear so that it can't move. In this scenario, when we turn the ring gear, the planets will "walk" along the sun gear (which is held stationary) causing the planet carrier to turn the output shaft in the same direction as the input shaft, but at a slower speed causing gear reduction (similar to a car in first gear).

If we unlock the sun gear and lock any two elements together, this will cause all three elements to turn at the same speed so that the output shaft will turn at the same rate of speed as the input shaft, like a car in third or high gear. Another way that we can use a planetary gear set is by locking the planet carrier from moving, then applying power to the ring gear which will cause the sun gear to turn in the opposite direction giving us reverse gear.

The illustration how the simple system described left would look in an actual transmission. The input shaft is connected to the ring gear, The output shaft is connected to the planet carrier which is also connected to a "multi-disk" clutch pack. The sun gear is connected to a drum which is also connected to the other half of the clutch pack. Surrounding the outside of the drum is a band that can be tightened around the drum when required to prevent the drum with the attached sun gear from turning.

The clutch pack is used, in this instance, to lock the planet carrier with the sun gear forcing both to turn at the same speed. If both the clutch pack and the band were released, the system would be in neutral. Turning the input shaft would turn the planet gears against the sun gear, but since nothing is holding the sun gear, it will just spin free and have no effect on the output shaft. To place the unit in first gear, the band is applied to hold the sun gear from moving. To shift from first to high gear, the band is released and the clutch is applied causing the output shaft to turn at the same speed as the input shaft.

Many more combinations are possible using two or more planetary sets connected in various ways to provide the different forward speeds and reverse that are found in modern automatic transmissions.

Some of the clever gear arrangements found in four, and now five, six and even seven-speed automatics are complex enough to make a technically astute lay person's head spin trying to understand the flow of power through the transmission, as it shifts from first gear through top gear while the vehicle accelerates to highway speed. On newer vehicles, the vehicle's computer monitors and controls these shifts, so that they are almost imperceptible.

Clutch Packs

A clutch pack consists of alternating disks that fit inside a clutch. Half of the disks are steel and have splines that fit into groves on the inside of the drum. The other half have a friction material bonded to their surface and have splines on the inside edge that fit groves on the outer surface of the adjoining hub. There is a piston inside the drum that is activated by oil pressure at the appropriate time to squeeze the clutch pack together so that the two components become locked and turn as one.

One-way Clutch

A one-way clutch (also known as a "sprag" clutch) is a device that allows a component such as ring gear to turn freely in one direction but not in the other. This effect is just like that of a bicycle, where the pedals will turn the wheel when pedaling forward, but will spin free when pedaling backward.

A common place where a one-way clutch is used is in first gear when the shifter is in the drive position. When you begin to accelerate from a stop, the transmission starts out in first gear. But have you ever noticed what happens if you release the gas while it is still in first gear? The vehicle continues to coast as if you were in neutral. Now, shift into low gear instead of drive. When you let go of the gas in this case, you will feel the engine slow you down just like a standard shift car. The reason for this is that in drive, a one-way clutch is used whereas in low, a clutch pack or a band is used.

Band

A band is a steel strap with friction material bonded to the inside surface. One end of the band is anchored against the transmission case while the other end is connected to a servo. At an appropriate time, hydraulic oil is sent to the servo under pressure to tighten the band around the clutch drum to stop the drum from turning.

Torque Converter

On automatic transmissions, the torque converter takes the place of the clutch found on standard shift vehicles. It is there to allow the engine to continue running when the vehicle comes to a stop. The principle behind a torque converter is like taking a fan that is plugged into the wall and blowing air into another fan which is unplugged. If you grab the blade on the unplugged fan, you are able to hold it from turning. But as soon as you let go, it will begin to speed up until it comes close to the speed of the powered fan. The difference of a torque converter is that instead of using air, it uses oil or transmission fluid, to be more precise.

A torque converter is a large doughnut shaped device (10 to 15 inch in diameter) that is mounted between the engine and the transmission. It consists of three internal elements that work together to transmit power to the transmission. The three elements of the torque converter are the pump, the turbine and the stator. The pump is mounted directly to the converter housing which in turn is bolted directly to the engine's crankshaft and tuns at engine speed. The turbine is inside the housing and is connected directly to the input shaft of the transmission providing power to move the vehicle. The stator is mounted to a one-way clutch so that it can spin freely in one direction but not in the other. Each of the three elements have fins mounted in them to precisely direct the flow of oil through the converter. With the engine running, transmission fluid is pulled into the pump, the fluid will make contact with the front of the stator fins which push the stator into the one way clutch and prevent it from turning. With the stator stopped, the fluid is directed by the stator fins to reenter the pump at a "helping" angle providing a torque increase. As the speed of the turbine catches up with the pump, the fluid starts hitting the stator blades on the back-side causing the stator to turn in the same direction as the pump and turbine. As the speed increases, all three elements begin to turn at approximately the same speed.

Since the 1980s, in order to improve fuel economy, torque converters have been equipped with a lockup clutch which locks the turbine to the pump as the vehicle speed reaches approximately 45~50 MPH. This lockup is controlled by computer and usually won't engage unless the transmission is in third or fourth gear.

Hydraulic System

The hydraulic system is a complex maze of passages and tubes that sends transmission fluid under pressure to all parts of the transmission and torque converter. The newer systems are much more complex and are combined with computerized electrical components. Transmission fluid serves a number of purposes including shift control, general lubrication and transmission cooling.

New Words

1. hydraulic [haɪˈdrɔlɪk] adj. 液压的
2. marvel [ˈmɑːrvl] n. 奇迹
3. loaf [loʊf] v. 游荡；运转
4. latch [lætʃ] n. 门闩；碰锁
5. hump [hʌmp] n. 隆起
6. transaxle [trænsˈæksl] n. 驱动桥
7. complexity [kəmˈplɛksɪti] n. 复杂(性)
8. gymnastics [dʒɪmˈnæstɪks] n. 技巧；体操
9. band [bænd] n. 带子
10. governor [ˈgʌvərnə(r)] n. 调速器
11. modulator [ˈmɑdʒəleɪtɚ] n. 调节器
12. appropriate [əˈproʊpriət] adj. 适当的
13. astute [əˈstuːt] adj. 机敏的
14. imperceptible [ˌɪmpərˈsɛptəbl] adj. 觉察不到的
15. sprag [spræg] n. 楔块
16. coast [koʊst] v. 沿海岸而行
17. servo [ˈsɜːrvoʊ] n. 伺服系统
18. doughnut [ˈdoʊˌnʌt,-nət] n. (轮胎等)环状物
19. maze [mez] n. 曲径；迷宫
20. passages [ˈpæsɪdʒz] n. 通道，通路
21. submerge [səbˈmɜːrdʒ] v. 浸没；淹没
22. anti-freeze [ˈæntiˌfriz] n. 防冻剂
23. quart [kwɔːrt] n. 夸脱(容量单位)
24. flange [flændʒ] n. 轮缘；凸缘
25. pan [pæn] n. 平底锅，盘子，面板
26. solenoid [ˈsoʊlənɔɪd] n. 螺线管
27. pinpoint [ˈpɪnˌpɔɪnt] n. 精确
28. seal [sil] n. 密封；密封衬垫
29. gasket [ˈgæskɪt] n. 垫圈；衬垫
30. windshield [ˈwɪndˌʃild] n. 挡风玻璃
31. cork [kɔːrk] n. 软木塞
32. manipulate [məˈnɪpjəlet] v. 操作
33. spinning [ˈspɪnɪŋ] n. 自转

Phrases and Expressions

1. RPM (revolutions per minute) 转/分
2. rear wheel drive 后轮驱动
3. real axle 后轴；后桥
4. torque converter 液力变扭器

5. the final drive 主减速器
6. drive shaft 传动轴
7. planetary gear set 行星齿轮组
8. sun gear 恒星齿轮,太阳轮
9. planet gears 行星齿轮,行星轮
10. ring gear 环形齿轮,齿圈
11. constant mesh 常啮合
12. one-way clutch 单向离合器
13. circulatory system 循环系统
14. pump element 泵芯子
15. be responsible for 为……负责;形成……的原因
16. gas pedal 加速踏板
17. leaking out 泄漏
18. aside from 除……以外
19. MPH (miles per hour) 英里/小时

Notes to Text

1. Automatic transmissions contain mechanical systems, hydraulic systems, electrical systems and computer controls, all working together in perfect harmony which goes virtually unnoticed until there is a problem.

自动变速器包含机械系统、液压系统、电气系统和计算机控制。所有这些系统在一起完美地协调工作,几乎不被察觉,直到出现问题。

2. On a rear wheel drive car, the transmission is usually mounted to the back of the engine and is located under the hump in the center of the floorboard alongside the gas pedal position.

在后轮驱动的汽车中,变速器通常安装在发动机后端,位于地板中心的驼峰下,与油门踏板位置并排。

3. In a manual transmission, gears slide along shafts as you move the shift lever from one position to another engaging various sized gears as required in order to provide the correct gear ratio. In an automatic transmission, however, the gears are never physically moved and are always engaged to the same gears.

在手动变速器中,当你将换挡杆从一个位置移到另一个位置时,各种大小的齿轮沿着轴滑动并相互啮合,以提供正确的齿轮比。然而,在自动变速器中,齿轮永远不会在位置上有所移动,而且总是与相同的齿轮啮合。

4. There is a piston inside the drum that is activated by oil pressure at the appropriate time to squeeze the clutch pack together so that the two components become locked and turn as one.

鼓内有一个活塞,在适当的时候被油压激活,将离合器包挤压在一起,使两者锁定为一体并转动。

5. A common place where a one-way clutch is used is in first gear when the shifter is in the drive position.

当变速器处于驱动位置时,单向离合器通常被使用在第一个齿轮上。

6. If we unlock the sun gear and lock any two elements together, this will cause all three elements to turn at the same speed so that the output shaft will turn at same rate of speed as the input shaft.

如果我们松开太阳齿轮,而把任何两个元件锁定,将导致所有三个元件以相同的速度旋

转,从而使输出轴与输入轴以相同的速率旋转。

Exercises

1. Answer the following questions to the text.

(1) What is an automatic transmission?
(2) What are the main components of an automatic transmission?
(3) What does a basic planetary gear set consist of?
(4) What are the three elements of the torque converter?
(5) What is the function of the hydraulic system?

2. Translate the following phrases and expressions into Chinese.

(1) rear drive wheel
(2) front axel
(3) planetary gear sets
(4) electrical solenoids
(5) clutch pack
(6) RPM and MPH

3. Translate the following sentences into Chinese.

(1) A drive shaft connects the rear of the transmission to the final drive which is located in the rear axle and is used to send power to the rear wheels.

(2) The pump is mounted directly to the converter housing which in turn is bolted directly to the engine's crankshaft and tuns at engine speed.

(3) When you begin to accelerate from a stop, the transmission starts out in first gear. But have you ever noticed what happens if you release the gas while it is still in first gear?

(4) A band is a steel strap with friction material bonded to the inside surface.

(5) The principle behind a torque converter is like taking a fan that is plugged into the wall and blowing air into another fan which is unplugged.

(6) The hydraulic system is a complex maze of passages and tubes that sends transmission fluid under pressure to all parts of the transmission and torque converter.

Part Ⅲ Listening and Speaking

Negotiation of Price A

A—Customer   B—Salesperson

A: How much is this new model 675?
B: It's 465,000 yuan.

A: I like this car very much, but it's a bit expensive for me. Can you give me a discount?
B: Well, this is the newest model and very popular. I think it's worth buying.
A: Yes, I know, but I think that still might be a little high for this car.
B: You could save a little bit if you choose to pay in cash.
A: Really? Tell me about it.
B: Well, we offer a 5% discount for cash payment.
A: I see. Other than that, could you please be able to come down on the price a little bit?
B: That's beyond my capability. I need to ask the manager about it. I'll let you know after I talk to him.
A: OK. Thank you very much!
B: You're welcome.

Negotiation of Price B

A—Customer   B—Salesperson

A: Why are there three prices quoted for this part?
B: They represent the prices for different quantities.
A: I see.
B: The more you order, the more you will save.
A: OK, got it. Let's discuss the terms of payment. Do you accept credit cards or I should pay in cash?
B: Either is OK.
A: That's very good. But is it OK if I pay by Banker's Transfer?
B: Sony, I'm afraid not. We accept payments in cash or by credit card only.
A: Oh, I don't think I have enough cash with me and I have no credit card.
B: Well, we have installment payment that can help you. The down payment is 1/3 of the price. The first installment should be paid a week before the shipment. The second one should be paid one day before the shipment. Then pay the last installment when you get the car.
A: That's great. I'll pay the down payment now.

Part IV   Reading Material

Continuously Variable Transmission

Development Situation

CVT (Continuously Variable Transmission) technology has been developed for over a hundred years in foreign countries. As early as in 1886, Mercedes-Benz began to apply rubber v-belt CVT in its automobiles.

The development course of CVT can be divided into three phases.

Phase One — The Exploration of CVT Technology

In the late 1970s, VDT (Van Doorne Transmission) Company in the Netherlands developed the first automotive CVT, named VDT-CVT. However, it was not widely accepted by the automobile industry because of its defects such as the limitation of transmit power, instability of the clutch, and energy loss in hydraulic pump, transmission belt and clamping mechanism caused by the use of rubber belt. At that time, a common gear transmission, fitting in with high power output, was in a dominant position in the market.

Phase Two — The Development of CVT Technology

In 1987, Subaru Company in Japan applied metal belt ECVT in its JUSTY. To overcome the defects caused by rubber belt transmission, after a series of studies on the performance of a transmission belt and the limit of transmit power, researchers integrated a torque converter into CVT system. The clamping force of the driving and driven wheel was electronically controlled. Energy-saving pump and metal belt instead of traditional rubber belt were also used.

Phase Three — The Maturation of CVT Technology

In 1990s, more and more attention was paid to research and development of CVT, which was considered to be the key technology especially in minicabs. The rapid development of global science and technology made new electronic and automatic control technology continuously adopted into CVT. In 1997, Nissan developed a new CVT with wide high-strength steel belt and high hydraulic control system for its 2.0-liter automobiles. Through the application of advanced technologies, torque transmission capacity can be improved, and the change of transmission ratio can be electronically controlled. This type of CVT can control the engine braking according to the speed when the vehicle going downhill, and increase the ratio smoothly to prevent skidding on slippery roads. In 1999, Ford cooperated with German ZF Company to manufacture CVT for its cars and light trucks. The CVT designed by ZF was a kind of torque-converter gearbox with a steel belt that was produced for transverse engine front-wheel driving automobiles. Compared with traditional automatic transmission, CVT system can improve acceleration by 10% and fuel economy by 10% to 15%.

Nowadays, all the major auto companies are energetically conducting researches on CVT in order to raise their competitiveness. In recent years, with the wide application of electronic technology, Germany and Japan have attached great importance to electronically controlled V-shaped metal belt CVT and developed their electronically controlled CVT.

Advantages of CVT

In the running process of a vehicle, the driver chooses a gear according to the change of speed and load. In that situation, the relationship between engine and speed is determined by the gear ratio of gear pairs. However, transmission of this kind cannot ensure power output and optimum fuel economy because of the inherent feature of internal combustion engine. Increasing the number of gears can help remedying the problem, but that will be restricted by the cost as well as the structure and weight of the gearbox. Conversely, one distinctive feature of CVT is that it can make engine speed and vehicle speed obtain corresponding continuous change, which will make full use of the characteristics of the engine and therefore optimally match the power of the vehicle with its fuel economy.

Unit 14　Steering System

Part Ⅰ　Illustrated English

Diagram of Steering System

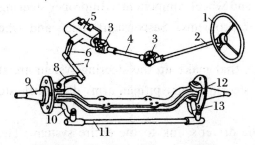

Fig. 14-1　Mechanical Steering System

1. steering wheel　转向盘
2. steering shaft　转向轴
3. steering universal joint　转向万向节
4. steering drive axle　转向传动轴
5. steering device　转向器
6. pitman arm　转向摇臂
7. steering drag link　转向直拉杆
8. knuckle arm　转向节臂
9./13. left steering knuckle　左转向节
10. track rod lever　梯形臂
11. steering tie-rod　转向横拉杆
12. right steering knuckle　右转向节

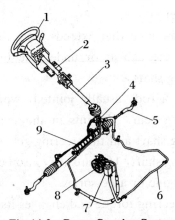

Fig. 14-2　Power Steering System

1. steering wheel　转向盘
2. steering shaft　转向轴
3. steering universal drive　转向万向传动装置
4. steering control valve　转向控制阀
5. steering tie-rod　转向横拉杆
6. oil pipe　油管
7. steering oil tank　转向油罐
8. steering hydraulic pump　转向液压泵
9. mechanical steering gear　机械转向器

Part II Technical and Practical Reading

Steering System

The steering system must deliver precise directional control. And it must do so requiring little driver effort at the steering wheel. Truck steering systems are either manual or power assisted, with power assist units using either hydraulic or air assist setups to make steering effort easier.

In addition to its vital role in vehicle control, the steering system is closely related to front suspension, axle, and wheel components. Improper steering adjustment can lead to alignment and tire wear problems. Suspension, axle, and wheel problem can affect steering and handing.

The key components that make up the steering system are steering wheel, steering column, steering shaft, steering gear, pitman arm, drag link, steering arm, ball joints, and tie-rod assembly.

Steering wheel is the driver's link to the entire system. The wheel is formed of a strong steel rod shaped into a wheel. Spokes extend from the wheel to the wheel hub, which is fastened securely at the top of the steering column. The wheel assembly is covered with rubber or plastic. The steering column transfers driver input to the steering gear. In other words, driver effort applied to the steering wheel at the rim becomes torque in the steering shaft. The larger the steering wheel diameter is, the more torque is generated from the same amount of drive effort. Most steering wheels on heavy-duty trucks are 22 inches in diameter.

Steering column is a hollow tube that extends from the steering wheel through the floorboard. It is fastened to the cab at or under the instrument panel and contains bearings to support the steering shaft.

Steering shaft is basically a rod, usually jointed, which runs from the top of the steering column to the steering gear. U-joints in the shaft accommodate any angular variations between the steering shaft and the steering gear input shaft. Usually found at one or both ends of the steering shaft, U-joints may also be used in the middle to route a multipiece shaft around the engine or accessories.

Steering gear multiplies steering torque and changes its direction as received through the steering shaft from the steering wheel. There are two widely used types of gears: worm and roller, and recirculating ball.

Pitman arm is a steel arm clamped to the output shaft of the steering gear. The outer end of the pitman arm moves through an arc in order to change the rotary motion of the steering gear output shaft into linear motion. The length of the pitman arm affects

Unit 14 Steering System

steering quickness. A longer pitman arm will generate more steering motion at the front wheels for a given amount of steering wheel movement.

Drag link forged rod connects the pitman arm to the steering arm. The drag link can be a one-piece or two-piece component. The two-piece design is adjustable in length, a fact that makes it easy to center the steering gear with the wheels straight ahead. One-piece drag link is used in systems with very close tolerances. Other components are used to make adjustments to the system when a one-piece drag link is used. The drag link is connected at each end by ball joints. These ball joints isolate the steering gear and pitman arm from axle motion.

Steering arm sometimes called steering lever; this forged steel component connects the drag link to the top portion of the driver's side steering knuckle and spindle. As the steering arm moves, it changes the angle of the steering knuckle and thus alters the direction in which the steering knuckle spindle is pointing.

Ball joints, called ball-and-socket assembly, consist of a forged steel ball with a threaded stud attached to it. A socket shell grips the ball. The ball stud moves around to provide the freedom of movement needed for various steering links to accommodate relative motion between the axle and the frame rail when the front axle springs flex. A ball stud is mounted in the end of each steering arm and provides the link between the drag link and the steering arm.

The steering arm or lever controls the movement of the driver's side steering knuckle. There must be some methods of transferring this steering motion to the opposite passenger side steering knuckle. This is done through the use of a tie-rod assembly that links the two steering knuckles together and forces them to act in unison. The tie-rod assembly is also called a cross tube.

New Words

1. steering ['stɪrɪŋ] n. 操纵，掌舵
2. precise [prɪ'saɪs] adj. 精确的，精密的；严谨的
3. effort ['efərt] n. 努力，作用力
4. alignment [ə'laɪnmənt] n. 调准
5. pitman ['pɪtmən] n. 连杆，摇杆
6. hub [hʌb] n. (轮)毂，中心
7. axle ['æksəl] n. (轮)轴，车桥
8. column ['kɑːləm] n. 圆柱，柱状物
9. spoke [spoʊk] n. (车轮上)辐条，阻碍物
10. rim [rɪm] n. 轮辋
11. floorboard ['flɔːrbɔːrd] n. 地板(总称)
12. hollow ['hɑːloʊ] adj. 中间空的，空洞的
13. worm [wɜːrm] n. 蜗杆
14. roller ['roʊlə(r)] n. 假定，推测
15. clamp [klæmp] n. 钳子
16. forge [fɔːrdʒ] vt. 锻造
17. stud [stʌd] n. 柱头螺栓
18. spindle ['spɪndl] n. 轴，芯轴
19. knuckle ['nʌkəl] n. 关节；勾爪

Phrases and Expressions

1. electrical system　电气系统
2. internal combustion engine　内燃机
3. combustible mixture　可燃混合物
4. steering system　转向系统
5. power assisted steering　助力转向
6. air assist setups　空气助力机构
7. steering wheel　转向盘，方向盘
8. steering column　转向管柱
9. steering shaft　转向轴
10. steering gear　转向器
11. pitman arm　转向摇臂
12. drag link　转向直拉杆
13. ball joint　球形接头
14. steering knuckle　转向节
15. ball-and-socket joint　球铰接
16. tie rod　转向横拉杆

Notes to Text

1. The larger the steering wheel diameter, the more torque is generated from the same amount of drive effort.

方向盘的直径越大，相同的驱动力所产生的力矩就越大。

2. Steering gear multiplies steering torque and changes its direction as received through the steering shaft from the steering wheel.

方向盘带动转向轴转动，转向齿轮增大了转向力矩从而改变汽车方向。

3. A longer pitman arm will generate more steering motion at the front wheels for a given amount of steering wheel movement.

对于特定的方向盘运动量来说，较长的摇臂将在前轮产生更多的转向运动。

4. Ball joints, called ball-and-socket assembly, consist of a forged steel ball with a threaded stud attached to it.

球头万向节，即滚珠和承窝组件，包括一个连接到其滚珠上的双头螺栓。

5. A ball stud is mounted in the end of each steering arm and provides the link between the drag link and the steering arm.

每个转向臂的末端都安装有一个球头螺栓，实现了拉杆和转向臂之间的连接。

Exercises

1. Answer the following questions to the text.

(1) What is the function of the automobile engine?

(2) Explain the function of the steering system, please.

(3) What are the key components that make up the steering system?

(4) What is the purpose of steering gear?

(5) What is the purpose of steering arm?

(6) What is the function of steering wheel?

2. **Translate the following phrases and expressions into Chinese.**

(1) steering system

(2) steering wheel

(3) steering column

(4) air assist setups

(5) ball-and-socket joint

(6) steering shaft

3. **Translate the following sentences into Chinese.**

(1) The key components that make up the steering system are steering wheel, steering column, steering shaft, steering gear, pitman arm, drag link, steering arm, ball joints, and tie-rod assembly.

(2) The steering column transfers driver input to the steering gear.

(3) It is fastened to the cab at or under the instrument panel and contains bearings to support the steering shaft.

(4) Pitman arm is a steel arm clamped to the output shaft of the steering gear.

(5) Drag link forged rod connects the pitman arm to the steering arm.

(6) A ball stud is mounted in the end of each steering arm and provides the link between the drag link and the steering arm.

Part Ⅲ Listening and Speaking

Maintenance A

A—Receptionist B—Customer

A: Hello. This is Sales Department, New Century Automobile Company.

B: I'm afraid I have to make a complaint about your corporation. It's a most unpleasant incident.

A: Oh, what is it about? I'm so sorry to hear that.

B: Yes, I ordered a set of wheel alignment the other day. I received it and then I examined them one by one. I found that there must be something wrong with the related computer because it can't give any signal. That's why I want to see the manager.

A: I am sure everything is all right with that shipment. You see I know you're our regular customer and it is the first time for me to meet with such an inconvenient thing.

B: I want to return this.

A: Without sufficient evidence to support, your claim is untenable. If we were at fault, we should be very glad to compensate for your loss.

B: What's your opinion?
A: I'm terribly sorry about that. May I know your name and address, sir? I'll check it and send a repairman to your side at once.
B: OK. Thank you!

Maintenance B

A—Receptionist   B—Customer   C—Service Manager

A: What's the matter?
B: I think something must be wrong with the computer for wheel alignment because there is no signal on the screen.
A: Oh, the engine went dead. We're so sorry to have caused you so much inconvenience and we have to replace it. Let me have a look at your warranty certificate.
B: Here it is.
A: Well, your warranty is expired. We have to charge for the parts.
B: That's all right. We're dying for the normal work condition at any expense.
A: It's OK. You can turn on the power now.
B: I appreciate your coming here in time.
A: If anything is wrong with your computer, don't hesitate to call us a moment and we're at your service.
B: Thank you.
A: My pleasure.
C: Hello. This is New Century Automobile Company. I'm calling to know whether everything has gone well with your computer.
B: Thanks a lot. It works excellently after being repaired.
C: I'm very happy to hear you say so and I do hope the minor problem didn't cause you much inconvenience.
B: Thank you very much for your good service. I'm sure your company will be making more money.
C: It is always our policy to give reliable and satisfactory services to our clients. If you have any further problems, please let us know. We shall be glad to hear from you.
B: OK. I will. Thank you!

Part Ⅳ   Reading Material

Types of Steering Gears

Steering gear is a device for converting the rotary motion of driver's steering wheel into the straight line motion of the linkages or angular turning of the front wheels. It consists of mainly two parts — a worm on the end of the steering shaft and a pitman arm shaft. There is a gear sector, a toothed roller or stud fitted on the pitman arm shaft.

There are different types of steering gears used on different vehicles. Depending upon the method of coupling the steering tube with the cross shaft, different types of steering gears are as follows: worm and roller, worm and sector, cam and roller, cam and peg, screw and nut, recirculating ball, worm and ball bearing, rack and pinion.

Worm and roller gear consists of a two-toothed-roller fastened to the cross shaft known as roller shaft, a sector shaft and a pitman shaft. At the end of the steering tube, it meshes with the threads of the worm gear. As it is turned by the steering tube, the roller is moved in an arc for rotating the roller shaft as well as turning on the pin connected the shaft. The roller is generally mounted on ball bearings or on some antifriction type of bearing. The control of the end float of the rocker shaft is by an adjusting screw due to a small offset of the roller to the worm. The bearings mounting the worm shaft are designed for resisting both radial and end thrust. Generally this steering gear is bolted to the frame.

Worm and sector gear consists of a casehardened steel worm and a sector located on bearings in a malleable iron or light alloy casting. The worm is connected to the inner column and the sector which form a part of the rocker shaft. This gear is also based on the principle of transmitting the motion from the steering tube to the pitman arm. It was developed from a worm and wheel-earliest design of steering gear.

Cam and roller gear consists of cam rotating in the housing, roller, rocker shaft and a drop arm. By moving the steering wheel and steering shaft, the cam is rotated. Due to this rotation, the roller is compelled to follow the helix of the groove. By this, the rocker shaft is caused to rotate as well as the drop arm is moved. In order to maintain the constant depths of mesh and evenly distributing the load and wear on the mating parts, the contour of the cam is properly designed to match the arm made by the roller.

Cam and peg gear consists of a tapered peg in the rocker arm engaging with a special cam formed on the inner column. By rotating the cam through the steering shaft, the peg is moved along the groove for rotating the rocker shaft. Shims control the end float of the column. In order to govern the backlash and end float of the rocker shaft, an adjusting screw on the side cover is used.

Screw and nut gear consists of a phosphor bronze of steel nut, screwed on to a multi-start; acme thread formed on the inner column. A ball fitted in the rocker arm prevents the rotation of the nut. A single ball race fitted at the top end of the rocker shaft takes up the axial thrust of the column while the lower end is supported by the nut sliding in the housing. The nut at the top end is used to adjust the end float of the inner column.

As the recirculating ball gear, if a nut with steel balls acting as threads is used in a worm and nut steering gear, a higher efficiency of 90% can be attained. This steering gear is an improved form of the worm and nut.

Worm and ball bearing gear using the principle of transmitting the motion from the steering tube to the pitman arm consists of a worm fitted on the lower end of the steering shaft and a ball nut mounted on it. The worm has mating spiral grooves in which steel balls circulate for providing frictionless drive between the worm and the nut. Generally two sets of balls are used with each set operating independently. The grooves in the worm and the ball nut and a ball-return guide attached to the outer surface of the nut are the components included in the circuit through which each set of balls circulates. The ball nut will be moved downward by the balls rolling between the worm and the nut when the steering shaft is turned to the left. The balls reaching the outer surface of the nut enter the return guides. Here they are directed across and down into the ball nuts to re-enter the circuit. The balls will circulate in the reverse direction due to the ball nut moving upward as a right turn is made. A sector gear or pitman shaft sector forged integral, with the pitman or cross shaft engages its teeth with the ball nut. In order to force the cross shaft to rotate, the teeth of the ball bearing nut moving up or down the shaft will move the sector teeth.

Rack and pinion gear has a rack acting as the centre section of a three-piece track rod. The rack having ball joints at each end for allowing the rise and fall of the wheels is engaged with the pinion mounted on the end of the steering shaft. The ball joints are further connected to the stub axles by rods. Sideways movements of the rack caused by the rotary movement of the steering wheel are directly conveyed to the wheels. The backlash in the rack is reduced to a minimum due to spring pads acting on the underside of the rack.

Unit 15 Suspension System

Part I Illustrated English

Diagram of Suspension System

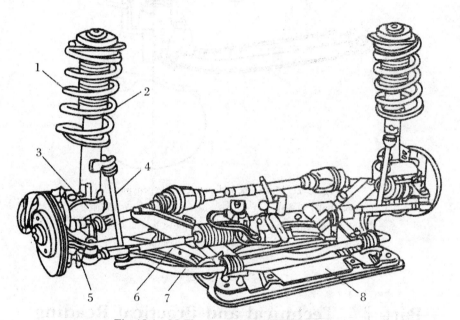

Fig. 15-1 McPherson Independent Suspension

1. coil spring 螺旋弹簧
2. cylindrical shock absorber 筒式减震器
3. steering knuckle 转向节
4. connecting link 连接杆
5. ball stud 球头销
6. lower sway arm 下摆臂
7. horizontal stabilizer Bar 横向稳定杆
8. front bracket 前托架

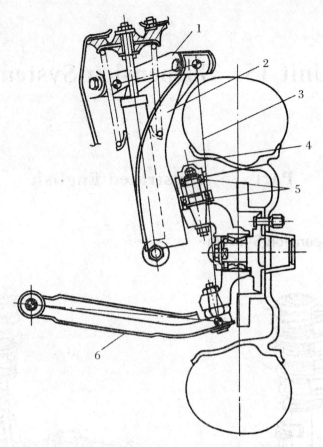

Fig. 15-2 Multi-ink Independent Suspension
1. upper link　上连杆
2. third connecting rod　第3连杆
3. axis of commutation　转向轴线
4. steering axis　主销轴线
5. thrust bearing　推力轴承
6. lower link　下连杆

Part Ⅱ　Technical and Practical Reading

Suspension System

The suspension system, while not absolutely essential to the operation of a motor vehicle, makes a big difference in the amount of pleasure experienced while driving. Essentially, it acts as a bridge between the occupants of the vehicle and the road they ride on.

As the wheels growl across the pavement, picking up a bump here, a crack there, the vibration travels up your legs and settles in your gut. You could almost admit you were having fun, if you didn't feel like you were gonna toss your tacos at any second. This is what your car would feel like without a suspension system.

Unit 15 Suspension System

As the suspension system, it has two basic principles of design: solid axle and independent suspension.

Solid axle suspension (also known as rigid axle) is the most elementary form of connecting the upper and the lower halves of a vehicle. As its name implies, it utilizes a single piece of metal — a common axle for both wheels sprung beneath the car's undercarriage. Pivots located between the axle and the wheel spindles allow the wheels to swivel on each end.

In solid axle suspension, because both wheels share the same axle, the up or down movement of one wheel causes a movement in the other wheel. They respond as one unit. As you can imagine, this doesn't make for the most comfortable ride. Even though solid axle designs utilize springs to soften their inherently harsh ride characteristics (more on different spring setups below), they still bump along like a brick outhouse. So why use them at all? Well, strength, for one. Because of the unitized construction, solid axle suspension systems offer incredible load bearing capacity. They also handle uneven roads superbly. You'll find in trucks.

The other main design is called independent suspension. As its name suggests, independent suspension assemblies offer a separate "bridge" for each wheel. They deliver the best ride characteristics by far, and are found most frequently in passenger cars, minivans, and other street vehicles. This is the most popular kind of suspension system in use today. If you like the "smoothness" of your car's ride, we can almost guarantee that it has independent suspension.

In addition to axles, wheels and tires, today's suspension systems utilize two other components that are critical to safe and comfortable driving: springs and shock absorbers.

Springs

A car's springs are the central part of the suspension. There are different designs of springs, such as torsion bars and leaf springs, but nearly all of today's passenger cars use coil springs at all four corners. A lot of trucks use coil springs too, with leaf springs for heavier load capacity typically found on a truck's rear suspension system.

Springs absorb and store road shock caused by bumps, dips, cracks, and so forth (remember the skateboard analogy). They absorb this shock by either compressing or extending. When a car's wheel goes over a bump and gets pushed upward, the spring absorbs that additional load, keeps the road shock from reaching the chassis, and makes sure the tire maintains contact with the pavement.

How much a spring compresses or extends is determined by its "spring rate". Spring rate is measured in pounds per inch of deflection, for example, 100 pounds per inch. So, say a load of 200 pounds is applied, the spring will deflect 2 inches. Spring rate comes from various factors. For a coil spring, it includes the number of the active coils, the diameter of the coils, and the diameter of the spring wire. The fewer coils a spring has, the higher the spring rate it will have.

The design of a spring affects how well the vehicle will ride and handle. A spring that absorbs lots of energy will generally offer a comfortable ride. After all, it can absorb most of the road shock (energy) that is being generated by the road surface. But there are always engineering trade-offs. This kind of spring generally requires a higher vehicle ride height, which will cause the vehicle to feel unstable during cornering. The more distance a spring compresses or extends, the more the vehicle "rolls" around on its suspension. This rolling is called weight transfer, and it is caused by centrifugal force acting on the weight of the vehicle as it goes around a corner. Weight transfer can overload a tire's grip, which ultimately hurts traction, and therefore handling.

Shock Absorbers

The other main part of a car's suspension is the shock absorber. Contrary to its name, a shock absorber plays a minimal role in absorbing impacts taken by the suspension. That's the spring's job. A shock absorber dampens road impacts by converting the up and down oscillations of the spring into thermal energy.

People who live and breathe don't like the term "shock absorbers"; they prefer "dampers". The unwashed masses — that's you and me — just call them shock absorbers. Without a shock absorber, a spring that has absorbed energy will release it by oscillating at an uncontrolled rate. The spring's inertia causes it to bounce and overextend itself. Then it recompresses, but again travels too far. The spring continues to bounce at its natural frequency until all the energy originally put into the spring is used up by friction. This effect can be quite detrimental to the stability of a vehicle.

Perhaps you've heard the word "strut". Struts are simply shock absorbers used as major structural members. For struts, the shock absorber is placed inside the coil spring. In addition to saving space, it often costs less. Many cars use a strut design.

Shocks and struts help control how fast the suspension is allowed to move, which is important for keeping the tires in contact with the road. Most shock absorber designs have more resistance during the extension (rebound) cycle than the compression cycle. This is because the extension cycle controls the motion of the vehicle's sprung weight (half of the suspension and everything else above the suspension). The compression cycle, on the other hand, controls the motion of unsprung weight (wheels, tires, brakes, and half of the suspension). Obviously, there is a lot more weight in the upper part of the car than unsprung weight in the lower part of the car.

New Words

1. suspension [sə'spenʃən] n. 悬挂
2. growl [graʊl] v. 发出隆隆声,咆哮
3. pavement ['pevmənt] n. 人行道
4. bump [bʌmp] v./n. 碰,颠簸;碰撞
5. crack [kræk] n. 裂缝;缝隙
6. vibration [vaɪ'breʃən] n. 振动,颤动

7. gut [gʌt] n. 内脏
8. axle ['æksəl] n. (轮)轴
9. rigid ['rɪdʒɪd] adj. 刚硬的, 刚性的
10. pivot ['pɪvət] n. 枢轴, 中心
11. spindle ['spɪndl] n. 轴
12. swivel ['swɪvəl] v. 旋转
13. like [laɪk] adj. 相似的, 同样的
14. harsh [hɑːʃ] adj. 刺耳的, 严厉的
15. uneven [ʌn'iːvən] adj. 不平坦的, 不平均的
16. minivan ['mɪnɪˌvæn] n. 小型货车
17. ride [raɪd] v./n. 乘坐, 骑; 乘车
18. dip [dɪp] n. 倾斜, 下降, 下沉; 浸渍
19. skateboard ['skeɪtbɔːrd] n. 滑板
20. analogy [ə'nælədʒɪ] n. 相似, 类比
21. deflection [dɪ'flɛkʃən] n. 转向, 偏斜
22. grip [grɪp] n. 紧; 掌握, 支配
23. oscillation [ˌɑːsɪ'leɪʃn] n. 振动
24. inertia [ɪ'nɜːrʃə] n. 惯性, 惯量
25. damper ['dæmpər] n. 减震器
26. bounce [baʊns] v. 弹回
27. frequency ['friːkwənsɪ] n. 频率
28. strut [strʌt] n. 支柱
29. unsprung [ʌn'sprʌŋ] adj. (车、椅等)不支承在弹簧上的, 未装弹簧的

Phrases and Expressions

1. suspension system 悬架系统
2. motor vehicle 汽车, 机动车
3. have fun 玩得开心
4. solid axle 实心轴, 固定轴
5. rigid axle type suspension 非独立悬架
6. independent suspension 独立悬架
7. torsion bar 扭杆弹簧
8. leaf spring 钢板弹簧
9. coil spring 螺旋弹簧
10. spring rate 弹簧刚度, 弹簧刚度系数
11. weight transfer 重量再分配, 重量转移
12. shock absorber 减震器

Notes to Text

1. The suspension system, while not absolutely essential to the operation of a motor vehicle, makes a big difference in the amount of pleasure experienced while driving.
虽然悬架系统对于汽车的运转并不是必需的, 但是当车辆行驶时它能使乘坐的舒适程度有很大的差异。

2. As the suspension system, it has two basic principles of design: solid axle and independent suspension.
悬架系统有两个基本的设计原则: 实心轴和独立悬架。

3. There are different designs of springs, such as torsion bars and leaf springs, but nearly all of today's passenger cars use coil springs at all four corners.
弹簧有不同的设计, 如扭杆弹簧和钢板弹簧, 但现在的小客车的四个车轮几乎都使用了螺旋弹簧。

4. A spring that absorbs lots of energy will generally offer a comfortable ride.
一个能吸收大量能量的弹簧通常会提供一个舒适的旅程。

5. Shocks and struts help control how fast the suspension is allowed to move, which

is important for keeping the tires in contact with the road.

冲击和压杆有助于控制悬架的速度,这对保持轮胎与路面的接触是非常重要的。

Exercises

1. Answer the following questions to the text.

(1) Why is the suspension system installed on a vehicle?

(2) What is two basic designs of the suspension system?

(3) What advantages does the independent suspension system have?

(4) What is the function of the springs of the suspension?

(5) What is the shock absorber's job?

2. Translate the following phrases and expressions into Chinese.

(1) coil spring

(2) spring rate

(3) solid axle

(4) weight transfer

(5) shock absorber

3. Translate the following sentences into Chinese.

(1) As the wheels growl across the pavement, picking up a bump here, a crack there, the vibration travels up your legs and settles in your gut.

(2) Solid axle suspension (also known as rigid axle) is the most elementary form of connecting the upper and the lower halves of a vehicle.

(3) In solid axle suspension because both wheels share the same axle, the up or down movement of one wheel causes a like movement in the other wheel.

(4) They deliver the best ride characteristics by far, and are found most frequently in passenger cars, minivans, and other street vehicles.

(5) There are different designs of springs, such as torsion bars and leaf springs, but nearly all of today's passenger cars use coil springs at all four comers.

(6) The spring continues to bounce at its natural frequency until all the energy originally put into the spring is used up by friction. This effect can be quite detrimental to the stability of a vehicle.

Part Ⅲ　Listening and Speaking

Steering system A

A—Student　B—Professor

A: Could you give me a brief account of the steering system?
B: Certainly. In fact, the steering system plays an important role in driving the car.
A: Well, what does the steering system consist of?
B: It mainly consists of steering wheel, steering gears, linkages and other components.
A: OK. What is the function of the steering system?
B: The steering system is used to control the direction of a car's motion and makes driving much more pleasurable, comfortable and safer.
A: Well, I see. Thanks for your information.
B: You are welcome.

Steering system B

A—Student   B—Professor

A: I heard that there are two basic types of steering systems on cars today. Would you like to tell me something in detail?
B: Sure. They are recirculating-ball steering and rack and pinion steering.
A: Any differences between them?
B: Yes. The recirculating-ball steering can be either power-assisted or non-power. But rack and pinion steering is almost always power-assisted. On the other hand, recirculating-ball steering is applied to many trucks and SUVs today. Most large automobiles are equipped with a recirculating-ball steering gear; however, rack and pinion steering mechanisms are used in many modern cars.
A: Well, what are their respective advantages?
B: The recirculating-ball steering is very low in friction and provides a good mechanical advantage for a heavy vehicle. It uses a series of links and arms to keep both wheels turning in the same direction at the same time.
A: How about rack and pinion steering?
B: The advantage of rack and pinion steering is relatively simple and the cost is low. And it has a much better direct steering feel for the driver. By reducing the number of parts and pivot points, it can control wheel direction more accurately.
A: I see, it is very kind of you to tell me so much.
B: My pleasure.

Part IV   Reading Material

Industry Overview

Along with the increase in automatic transmission cars, China's development prospects of the traditional clutch industry growing concern, many companies are seeking new ways of sustainable development. Prior to 2007, China's vehicle production continuing to grow, the increase in car ownership and export market demand, the three major factors promote the development of China's automotive clutch industry for 8 consecutive years rapidly. In 2007, China's output of clutch broke 10 million units. Since 2008, the global financial crisis, China's vehicle sales to 9.38 million, only 6.7% growth rate, the market size of clutch is about 5.5 billion. In 2010, China's auto market would bottom out, then the clutch total sales could be expected to exceed 8 billion yuan.

DCT technology's good prospects in China will bring new development opportunities to China friction plate clutch industry. However, the market competition is fierce. Changchun Yidong Clutch, the leading domestic auto clutch manufacturing industry, has formed the productivity of 750,000 sets, which is the largest and widest series of clutch manufacturers. Therefore, the industry status is higher. Company is in the OE Market Supporting the market in the host ranks, 64 OE supplier for the country, occupied the domestic medium and heavy commercial vehicle market in half.

Dual mass flywheel clutch is a traditional development direction. Our country has Luk, Excedy and other foreign companies in China, assembling dual-mass flywheel. Jilin Dahua, Hubei Tri-ring of the double mass flywheel have also entered the industrialization stage, but dual mass flywheel development prospects in China still subject to further market validation.

The demand of torque converter is increasing with the increase of the proportion of China's automatic transmission. Domestically, Shanghai Sachs had torque converter products long ago. Guangzhou Youdajia, Shanghai Excedy, Nanjing valeo and other foreign companies already have begun to assembly torque converter. Since the localization of AT technology is very difficult to develop, developing torque converter for the domestic enterprises still has higher risk.

Unit 16　Braking System

Part I　Illustrated English

Diagram of Braking System and ABS

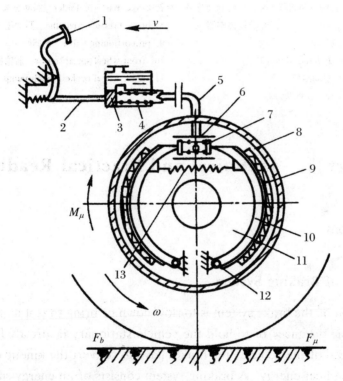

Fig. 16-1　Diagram of Working Principle of Brake System

1. brake pedal　制动踏板
2. push rod　推杆
3. master cylinder piston　主缸活塞
4. brake master cylinder　制动主缸
5. oil pipe　油管
6. wheel braking cylinder　制动轮缸
7. wheel cylinder piston　轮缸活塞
8. brake drum　制动鼓
9. friction disk　摩擦片
10. brake shoe　制动蹄
11. brake bottom plate　制动底板
12. rest button　支承销
13. brake shoe return spring　制动蹄回位弹簧

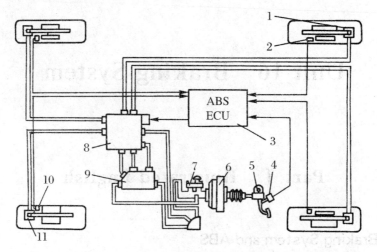

Fig. 16-2 Diagram of Composition and Control Principle of ABS

1. rear wheel brake branch pump　后轮制动分泵
2. rear wheel speed sensor　后轮速度传感器
3. controller　控制器
4. braking light switch　制动灯开关
5. brake pedal　制动踏板
6. vacuum booster　真空助力器
7. brake master cylinder　制动总泵
8. brake pressure machine　制动压力调机器
9. proportioning valve　比例阀
10. front wheel speed sensor　前轮速度传感器
11. front wheel brake branch pump　前轮制动分泵

Part II　Technical and Practical Reading

Braking System

Basic Features of Braking System

The function of the brake system is to slow down or bring to rest a moving vehicle in a shortest possible distance, or to hold the vehicle stationary if already halted. In order to reduce the speed of the vehicle, the brakes have to convert the kinetic energy stored in the vehicle to the heat energy. A braking system consists of an energy-supplying device, a control device, a transmission device and the brake.

There are two completely independent brake systems used on a car: the service braking system and the parking braking system.

The service braking system is foot-operated by the driver depressing and releasing the brake pedal. It is used to stop or slow down your car during normal driving. It is also called running or foot brake.

The parking braking system is hand-operated. Its purposes are to hold a car stationary while it is unattended, and to keep the car from rolling on unleveled ground.

It controls the rear brakes through a series of steel cables that are connected to a hand level. It is also called the hand brake.

Types of Brakes

Basically, all car brakes are friction brakes. Two types of brakes are used in modern cars: drum brakes and disc brakes. In recent decades, all cars have used disc brakes on the front wheels. Drum brakes are cheaper to produce for the rear wheels.

Drum brakes consist of a back plate, brake shoes, brake drum, wheel braking cylinders, return springs and an automatic or self-adjusting system. Drum brakes employ two brake shoes mounted on a stationary backing plate. These shoes are positioned inside a circular drum which rotates with the wheel assembly.

When you apply the brakes, brake fluid is forced, under pressure into the wheel cylinder which pushes the brake shoes into contact with the machined surface on the inside of the drum. When the pressure within the wheel cylinder is released, return springs pull the shoes back to their rest position.

As the brake linings wear, the shoes must travel a greater distance to reach the drum. When the distance reaches a certain point, a self-adjusting mechanism automatically reacts by adjusting the rest position of the shoes so that they are closer to the drum.

Disk brakes, used for years for front wheel applications, are fast replacing drum brakes on the rear wheels of modern cars because of their simpler design and lighter weight and better resistance to "brake fade".

Disc brakes radiate the heat to the air better than drum brakes, so they have a greater resist-ante to fade (fall-off in brake efficiency due to heat) than the drum brake.

Compared with drum brake, the disk brake has a caliper (which is mounted rigidly and does not move), a metal disk or rotor (which is mounted on the hub) instead of a drum, and a pair of pads, or flat shoes, instead of the curved shoes. There are two general types of disk brakes: fixed caliper and floating caliper.

The fixed caliper design uses two pistons mounted on either side of the caliper (in each side of the rotor). When the brakes are applied, hydraulic pressure forces the pistons against the brake pads. This action forces the linings against the disk friction surfaces. Friction between the pads and the disk slows the disk down. The brake action occurs very quickly, because there is very small clearance between the brake linings and the disk surfaces.

Many latter model vehicles are equipped with single-piston floating calipers which are least costly to manufacture and service. A floating caliper "floats" or moves in a track in its support so that it can center itself over the rotor. As you apply brake pressure, the hydraulic fluid pushes in two directions. It forces the opposite direction against the inner pad which in turn pushes against the rotor. It also pushes the caliper in the opposite direction against the outer pad, pressing it against the outer side of the rotor. The force on each brake pad is equal. Floating calipers are also available on some vehicles with two pistons mounted on the side. Two-piston-floating calipers are found on more expensive cars and can provide an improved braking "feel".

Advantages over drum brakes are: much better gradual braking efficiency; equal wear of the in-board and outboard brake pads if the proper degree of heat dissipation is provided; brake noise is better suppressed; relatively constant brake factor performance with lower susceptibility to fading.

Hydraulic System

In terms of their power sources, brakes are basically of two types: the mechanically actuated brakes and the hydraulic brakes.

The mechanical brakes are mainly used in the parking brake. The parking system is full mechanical and completely bypasses the hydraulic system so that the vehicle can be brought to a stop even if there is a total brake failure. The hydraulic systems are used to actuate the drum and disc brakes of small cars. The typical hydraulic brake system consists of disk brakes on the front and either disk or drum brakes on the rear wheels connected by a system of tubes and hoses that link the brake at each wheel to the master cylinder.

The master cylinder is fluid-filled and contains two separate sections. There is a piston in each section and both pistons are connected to a brake pedal, converts driver foot's mechanical pressure.

When the brake pedal is pushed down, the two pistons move in the two sections of the master cylinder. This forces brake fluid out and through the brake lines, or tubes, to the brake mechanisms at the wheels. At the wheels, the fluid pushes shoes or pads against revolving drums or disks.

The brake fluid travels from the cylinder to the wheel through a series of steel tubes and reinforced rubber hoses. Rubber hoses are only used in places that require flexibility, such as at the front wheels. The rest of the system uses non-corrosive seamless steel tubing with special fittings at all attachment points.

The brake fluid is special oil that has special properties. It is designed to withstand cold temperatures without thickening as well as very high temperatures without boiling. It is very important that the fluid is pure liquid and that there is no air bubbles in it. Air can compress which causes sponginess to the pedal and severely reduced braking efficiency.

In order to ensure the efficiency of the brake system, the dual master cylinder is designed for both front and rear brakes of most cars. Double type master cylinders are designed to separate the front and the rear braking systems. The brake fluid from one section of the master cylinder goes to the two front-wheel brakes. The brake fluid from the other section goes to the two rear-wheel brakes. If brake fluid leak should occur in one system, the other system would still provide braking, making it possible to stop the car.

Antilock Brake Systems (ABS)

In a conventional brake system, if the brake pedal is depressed excessively, the wheels can lock up before the vehicle comes to a stop. When this happens, driver control is reduced. Research has shown that the quickest stops occur when the wheels are prevented from lockup.

The amount of lockup on a tire is referred to as slip. When a tire locks up completely during a stop, there is 100% slip. When a tire is rolling freely, there is 0% slip. Through research, it has been found that maximum braking force is generated when the tire slips about 10%~30%. This means that some tire rotations are necessary to achieve maximum braking.

Today, most vehicles use antilock braking systems. Antilock braking systems (ABS) are designed to prevent wheel lockup under heavy braking conditions on any type of road condition. The result is that, during heavy braking, the driver: retains directional stability (control of steering), stops faster, retains maximum control of the vehicle.

Under normal conditions, the ABS on a vehicle operates in much the same way as standard brake systems with a split or dual master cylinder. If, during braking, wheel lockup occurs, the system will enter the antilock mode. When the braking system is in this mode, hydraulic pressure is released on the wheel that is locking up. The amount of pressure released controls the wheel slip about 10%~30%, thus preventing lockup.

Antilock braking systems have various input and output components. The basic components of an antilock braking system include the wheel sensors, pressure modulator assembly, the master cylinder, and an electronic brake control module (EBCM) (computer).

A wheel speed sensor is located at each wheel. Its purpose is to sense the speed of each wheel. The speed is converted to an electrical signal and sent to the computer, often called the EBCM.

The pressure modulator assembly controls or modulates the hydraulic pressure to each wheel. The pressure modulator assembly contains the wheel circuit modulator valves used to control or modulate the hydraulic pressure to the brake calipers.

The pressure modulator assembly also contains a hydraulic pump motor. The pump motor takes low-pressure brake fluid from the fluid reservoir and pressurizes it for storage in an accumulator or for direct use in the antilock braking system. When the pressure on a caliper has been released because of an impending wheel lockup, pressure must be restored. The result is the production of a pulsing effect on the brakes. The pump motor helps to provide this extra buildup or increase in pressure.

An ABS master cylinder works the same as that on a standard braking system. During antilock condition, it works with the pressure modulator assembly to control or modulate the hydraulic pressure to the calipers on each wheel.

The EBCM is a small control computer that receives wheel speed information. On the basis of the wheel speed information, the EBCM sends an electronic signal to the pressure solenoids. The solenoids then control the hydraulic pressure to the calipers.

In some cars, EBCM is located in the trunk between the rear seat and the rear bulkhead trim panel. The primary functions of the EBCM are to detect wheel locking tendencies, control the brake system while in antilock mode, monitor the system for proper operation, and control the display of fault codes while in the diagnostic mode.

Other ABS components include fluid pressure sensors, pressure accumulators, pressure switches, piston travel switches, warning lamps, and self-diagnostic function check modes in the EBCM.

Various inputs and outputs are used in conjunction with the EBCM.

There are generally four modes of operation during antilock braking, including normal condition, pressure hold condition, pressure drop condition, and pressure release condition.

The normal condition mode operates when all four wheels are braking or slowing down equally. The other three conditions (pressure hold, pressure drop condition, and pressure increase condition) work when the computer senses an impending lockup. The cycle of pressure hold, pressure drop, and pressure increase occurs very rapidly, from 3 to 20 times per second.

New Words

1. kinetic [kɪˈnɛtɪk, kaɪ-] adj. 动力（学）的，运动的
2. hydraulic [haɪˈdrɔlɪk] adj. 液力的，液压的
3. indicator [ˈɪndɪˌketɚ] n. 指示器，示功器
4. caliper [ˈkæləpər] n. 卡钳
5. piston [ˈpɪstən] n. 活塞
6. backplate [ˈbækpleɪt] n. 背板
7. resistance [rɪˈzɪstəns] n. 抵抗，抗拒，抵御
8. clearance [ˈklɪrəns] n. 公隙；余隙，间隙
9. susceptibility [səˌsɛptəˈbɪlɪti] n. 敏感性；敏感度，灵敏度
10. actuate [ˈæktʃuˌet] v. 开动（机械等），驱使
11. reservoir [ˈrɛzɚvwɑː(r)] n. 贮液池，贮油器
12. reinforce [ˌriːɪnˈfɔːrs] v. 增强，加固
13. sponginess [ˈspʌndʒɪnəs] n. 海绵状，海绵质

Phrases and Expressions

1. brake booster 制动助力器
2. master cylinder 主缸
3. disc brake 盘式制动器
4. brake pad 制动块
5. brake disc 制动盘
6. service brake 行车制动

Unit 16 Braking System

7. parking brake　驻车制动
8. brake pedal　制动踏板
9. hand brake　手制动器
10. drum brake　鼓式制动器
11. brake lining　制动衬片
12. brake shoe　制动蹄
13. wheel cylinder　轮缸
14. brake hose　制动系统管路
15. anchor pin　定位销
16. leading shoe　领蹄
17. trailing shoe　从蹄
18. return spring　复位弹簧
19. brake fluid　制动液
20. brake fade　制动衰减
21. wheel hub　轮毂
22. fixed caliper　固定钳
23. floating caliper　浮钳

Notes to Text

1. There are two completely independent brake systems used on a car: the service braking system and the parking braking system.
汽车上使用的完全独立的制动系统有行车制动系统和驻车制动系统。

2. In order to ensure the efficiency of the brake system, the dual master cylinder is designed for both front and rear brakes of most cars.
为了保证制动系统的效率，大部分汽车的前后制动器设计了双主缸。

3. An ABS master cylinder works the same as that on a standard braking system.
ABS 制动系统的主缸与标准制动系统的是一样的。

4. The normal condition mode operates when all four wheels are braking or slowing down equally.
四个轮子都是制动或减速状态时，系统运行正常状态模式。

5. Various inputs and outputs are used in conjunction with the EBCM.
与 EBCM 连接的输入和输出形式是多种多样的。

Exercises

1. Answer the following questions to the text.
   (1) What are the main functions of the braking system?
   (2) How is the service brake operated?
   (3) Which advantages do disc brakes have over drum brakes?
   (4) What does the typical hydraulic brake system consist of?

2. Translate the following phrases and expressions into Chinese.
   (1) master cylinder
   (2) service brake
   (3) anchor pin
   (4) trailing shoe
   (5) floating caliper

3. Translate the following sentences into Chinese.

(1) The function of the brake system is to slow down or bring to rest a moving vehicle in a shortest possible distance, or to hold the vehicle stationary if already halted.

(2) In recent decades, all cars have used disc brakes on the front wheels, drum brakes are cheaper to produce for the rear wheels.

(3) The master cylinder are fluid-filled and contains two separate sections, there is a piston in each section and both pistons are connected to a brake pedal, converts driver foot's mechanical pressure.

(4) The amount of lockup on a tire is referred to as slip. When a tire locks up completely during a stop, there is 100% slip.

(5) Other ABS components include fluid pressure sensors, pressure accumulators, pressure switches, piston travel switches, warning lamps, and self-diagnostic function check modes in the EBCM.

Part Ⅲ Listening and Speaking

Crash Sensor A

A—Student   B—Professor

A: Excuse me, Professor, can you tell me some information about the crash sensor?
B: Definitely.
A: What is the crash sensor? And where is it located?
B: Crash sensor is one of the three basic parts in the airbag system. It is the device that tells the bag to inflate. They are located either in the front of the vehicle or in the passenger compartment, and play a crucial role in driving.
A: What functions do they perform?
B: They can be activated by forces generated in significant frontal or near-frontal crashes. In this way, the airbag is inflated and protects your head, neck, and chest from slamming against the dashboard, steering wheel of windshield, and significantly reduces the risk of serious to fatal injury in crashes.
A: Well, I know. Thank you very much for your valuable explanation.
B: My pleasure.

Crash Sensor B

A—Student   B—Professor

A: Excuse me, can you help me?

B: Certainly.
A: Do you have any ideas about SRS? And what is SRS short for?
B: Yes, SRS is short for Supplemental Restraint System.
A: Oh, I know. Well, what is the main job of SRS?
B: The main job of SRS is to help stop the passenger while doing as little damage to him as possible.
A: What does SRS consist of?
B: It consists of safety airbag and safety belt.
A: Is SRS airbag a complex part? How does it work?
B: Yes. In my opinion, it is quite complex. In an impact, sensors in the car detect the sudden deceleration. If the crash is serious, electricity flows to the inflator and causes ignition of the gas generator. And then the gas generator rapidly burns in the metal chamber, and after that, inert gases and small amounts of dust are produced. During inflation of the airbag, they are cooled and filtered.
A: Oh, complicated indeed. What is the next step?
B: Well, the inflating airbag splits open the trim cover. The airbag then quickly unfolds and inflates in front of the occupant.
A: Oh, I see. Thanks for your help.
B: You are welcome.

Part IV Reading Material

How F1 Brakes Work

Some of you are probably wondering how do Formula One cars, of 200 mph (321 km/h), manage to brake so effectively at the end of a long straight. The high temperatures reached the brake discs are enormous — sometimes exceeding 1,000 degrees Celsius — so how do they manage to build those things that are able to sustain hundreds of brakes per race?

In order to see how a regular Make system works, you're very welcome to visit our How Brakes Work article in the Guide section. Having said that, let's now focus on Formula One brakes, as they work on almost the same principle as in road cars, only they are made of different materials and undergo important changes in order to function at incredibly high temperatures.

First of all, the most important thing about an F1 braking system is that it is based on brake discs. During the course of their implementation in the Great Circle, the brake discs have been built out of steel, but time proves that carbon-made brake discs are certainly the safer and most effective way to go.

With both brake disc and caliper being made out of carbon fibre, it is ensured that the brakes will last at temperatures exceeding 1,000 degrees Celsius. A Formula One brake disc is 28 mm in thickness and 278 mm in diameter, and is made out of the best, possible carbon fibre, there is on the market. In fact, the construction of such a brake disc can take a manufacturer no less than half of year.

The building process of the carbon fibers used for brake discs & calipers is as follows: one takes the regular PAN (white polyacrylo nitrile) fibres and pre-oxidizes them via a heating process. However, this is only the first part of the forming process, as the outcome of this maiden stage is later carbonized. Following the carbonization, the resulted material has to spend days up to weeks into high-temperature ovens (simulating the temperatures during the race, meaning somewhere around 1,000 degrees Celsius), while combined with a hydrocarbon-rich gas. In this way, the carbon fibre layers inside the oven will merge perfectly in order to create one fine piece of brake disc.

The final stage of the process is cutting the resulted material into the form of a brake disc, depending on the system used by each team in particular. F1 teams might also opt for different manufacturing companies, with Hitco, Brembo and Carbon Industries being on top of the preference list.

Now that we've got this covered, let's have a look at how the system really works. As compared to road cars, Formula One machineries have their braking system divided into front braking and rear braking, as ruled by the International Automobile Federation. The reason for that bifurcation of the braking system is related to safety issues, meaning should one of the system fail to work properly, the next one can be activated in order to slow the car down.

In addition to that function, the separation of the front & the rear system allows the drivers to make use of brakes differently during the race. While most of the braking happens in the front end of the car, wet races (for example) require more efficient braking at the rear of the car. Also, being able to switch braking on front/rear also helps the drivers to preserve the tires against intense wear.

Two brake master cylinders from which brake fluid is pumped into the calipers cylinders of both front and rear brake systems are located inside the suspension, in order to maximize the space within the car's chassis. When the driver pushes the brakes, the forementioned fluid is inserted into the caliper's cylinders and leads to the contraction of the carbon brake block (located on the brake discs).

What's interesting about F1 braking is that the system is not activated at the exact time the driver pushes the brakes. In fact, for the first hundreds of a second — it may sound a very short period of time but, in F1 terms, it's translated into a considerable amount of time — the car behaves as if the brakes were not activated at all. The reason why that happens is that the process by which the brake discs and calipers come together needs to reach the best operating temperature — around 600 degrees Celcius. The braking temperatures grow 100 degrees Celsius every tenth of a second until half of second, as showed by *f1technical.net*.

After half of second passed, the temperatures exceed 1,000 degrees Celsius, causing the car to brake instantly, which is actually the downside of the whole thing, as the deceleration is quite brutal on the drivers. Just to make an idea of it, a driver undergoes a horizontal force close to 5.4 G when braking, as a F1 car can decelerate from 200 mph to a complete halt in only 4 seconds.

The second important part of a braking system for F1 machineries is the cooling system. We have to admit, no matter the material of which the disc brake is made of, it cannot withstand the high temperatures described above without constant cooling. Formula One team has used several solutions to improve cooling for the brakes, with the most important feature being the air ducts.

Air ducts are those little inlets created by the F1 mechanics in order to direct airflow towards the caliper and inside of the brake disc (located inside the wheel). In order to improve the airflow coming from outside the wheel, most teams have proceeded to fitting their rims with static wheel fairings. While also improving airflow around the car — as an aerodynamic effect — the forementioned feature also directs air straight into the brakes, while also securing improved brake exhaust airflow. The implementation of grooved brake discs is also aimed at keeping the brakes up to working temperatures.

Unit 17 Sensors

Part Ⅰ Illustrated English

Diagram of Sensors of Automobile Engine and Power System

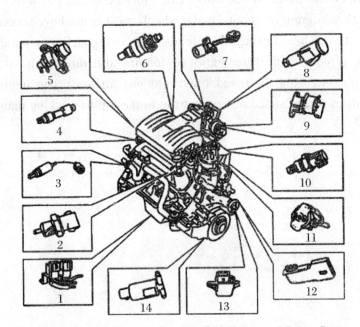

Fig.17-1 Sensor Locations of Automobile Engine and Power System

1. air bypass solenoid valve 空气旁路电磁阀
2. coolant temperature sensor 冷却液温度传感器
3. oxygen sensor 氧传感器
4. vehicle speed sensor 车速传感器
5. exhaust gas recirculation valve 废气再循环阀
6. injector 喷油器
7. throttle position sensor 节气门位置传感器
8. idle air bypass valve 怠速空气旁通阀
9. exhaust gas recirculation valve 废气再循环阀
10. intake air temperature sensor 进气温度传感器
11. crankshaft position sensor 曲轴位置传感器
12. ignition module 点火模块
13. manifold absolute pressure sensor 歧管绝对压力传感器
14. activated carbon canister 活性炭罐

Part Ⅱ Technical and Practical Reading

Sensors

Today's cars are riddled with sensors providing critical data for performance and safety. Initially, sensors were the first link in the signal path that monitors engine and drive-train parameters, such as oxygen, fluids, temperatures, voltages, and currents, but their usage soon expanded to the feedback loop from various actuators and motors, including antilock-brake systems and power-window motors.

The application of sensors is not limited solely to critical auto operation and safety factors or to reporting to the OnBoard-Diagnostics (OBD) system mandated for cars. As OEM confidence in sensors has increased along with sensor capabilities and reliability and sensor costs have decreased, sensors are now taking on more varied roles in the passenger compartment—for safety, comfort, convenience, and overall cocooning. But the following sensors are common in automobiles.

Oxygen Sensor

The ECM uses an oxygen sensor to ensure the air/fuel ratio is correct for the catalytic converter. Based on the oxygen sensor signal, the ECM will adjust the amount of fuel injected into the intake air stream. There are different types of oxygen sensors, but two of the more common types are the narrow range oxygen sensor and the wide range oxygen sensor.

The narrow range oxygen sensor is called the oxygen sensor simply. This oldest style of oxygen sensor has been in service for the longest time. The oxygen sensor generates a voltage signal based on the amount of oxygen in the exhaust compared to the atmospheric oxygen.

The wide range oxygen sensor is called the air/fuel ratio (A/F) sensor. It is the newest style. The air/fuel ratio (A/F) sensor is similar to the narrow range oxygen sensor. It is also referred to as a wide range or wide ratio sensor because of its ability to detect air/fuel ratio over a wide range. The advantage of using the A/F sensor is that the ECM can more accurately meter the fuel reducing emissions. To accomplish this, the A/F sensor operates at approximately 650 ℃, much hotter than the oxygen sensor 400 ℃. It changes its current (amperage) output in relation to the amount of oxygen in the exhaust stream.

Air Flow Sensor

The Mass Air Flow (MAF) sensors convert the amount of air drawn into a voltage signal. The ECM needs to know intake air volume to calculate engine load. This is necessary to determine how much fuel to inject, when to ignite the cylinder, and when to shift the transmission. The air flow sensor is located directly in the intake air stream, between the air cleaner and the throttle body where it can measure incoming air.

The primary components of the MAF sensor are a thermistor, a platinum hot wire, and an electronic circuit. The thermistor measures the temperature of the coming air. The hot wire is maintained at a constant temperature in relation to the thermistor by the electronic control circuit. An increase in air flow will cause the hot wire to lose heat faster and the electronic control circuit will compensate by sending more current through the wire. The electronic control circuit simultaneously measures the current flow and puts out a Voltage Signal (VS) in proportion to current flow.

The vane air flow meter provides the ECM with an accurate measure of the load placed on the engine. The ECM uses it to calculate basic injection duration and basic ignition advance angle.

Temperature Sensor

The ECM needs to adjust a variety of systems based on temperature. It is critical for proper operation of these systems that the engine reaching operating temperature and the temperature is accurately signed to the ECM. Temperature sensors measure Engine Coolant Temperature (ECT), Intake Air Temperature (IAT) and Exhaust Recirculation Gases (ERG), etc.

The ECT responds to change in engine coolant temperature. By measuring engine coolant temperature, the ECM knows the average temperature of the engine. The ECT is usually located in a coolant passage just before the thermostat.

The IAT detects the temperature of the coming air stream. On vehicles equipped with a MAP sensor, the IAT is part of the MAF sensor. The IAT is used for detecting ambient temperature on a cold start and intake air temperature as the engine heats up the incoming air.

The ERG temperature sensor is located in the ERG passage and measures the temperature of the exhaust gases. When the ERG valve opens, temperature increases. From the increase in temperature, the ECM knows the ERG valve is open and that exhaust gases are flowing.

Though these sensors are measuring different things, they all operate in the same way. From the voltage signal of the temperature sensor, the ECM knows the temperature. As the temperature of the sensor heats up, the voltage signal decreases. The decrease in the voltage signal is caused by the decrease in resistance. The change in resistance causes the voltage signal to drop. From the voltage signal, the ECM can determine the temperature of the coolant, intake air, or exhaust gas temperature.

Vehicle Speed Sensor (VSS)

The ECM uses the Vehicle Speed Sensor (VSS) signal to modify engine function and initiate diagnostic routines. The VSS signal originates from a sensor measuring transmission/transaxle output speed or wheel speed. Different types of sensors have been used depending on models and applications.

EGR Valve Position Sensor

The EGR valve position sensor is mounted on the EGR valve and detects the height of the EGR valve. The ECM uses this signal to control EGR valve height. The EGR valve position sensor converts the movement and the position of the EGR valve into an electrical signal.

Manifold Absolute Pressure Sensor

In the Manifold Absolute Pressure (MAP) Sensor there is a silicon chip inside a reference chamber. On one side of the chip is a reference pressure, depending on the application. On the other side is the pressure to be measured. The silicon chip changes its resistance with the changes in pressure. When the silicon chip flexes with the change in pressure, the electrical resistance of the chip changes. This change in resistance alters the voltage signal. The ECM interprets the voltage signal as pressure and any change in the voltage signal means there was a change in pressure.

Intake manifold pressure is a directly related engine load. The ECM needs to know intake manifold pressure to calculate how much fuel to inject, when to ignite the cylinder, and other functions. The MAP sensor is located either directly on the intake manifold or it is mounted high in the engine compartment and connected to the intake manifold with vacuum hose.

Vapor Pressure Sensor

The Vapor Pressure Sensor (VPS) measures the vapor pressure in the evaporative emission control system. The vapor pressure sensor maybe located on the fuel tank, near the charcoal canister assembly, or in a remote location. This sensor operates the same as the MAP sensor except that it measures the vapor pressure in the evaporative emission control system.

Barometric Pressure Sensor

The Barometric Pressure Sensor, sometimes called a High Altitude Compensator (HAC), measures the atmospheric pressure. This sensor operates the same as the MAP sensor expect that it measures the atmospheric pressure. It is located inside the ECM. If it is defective, the entire ECM must be replaced.

Knock Sensor

The knock sensor detects engine knock and sends a voltage signal to the ECM. The ECM uses the knock sensor signal to control timing.

Engine knock occurs within a specific frequency range. The knock sensor, located in the engine block, cylinder head, or intake manifold, is tuned to detect that frequency. Inside the block sensor, there is a piezoelectric element. The piezoelectric element in the knock sensor is tuned to the engine knock frequency. The vibrations from engine knocking vibrate piezoelectric element generating a voltage. The voltage output from the knock sensor is the highest at this time.

New Words

1. riddle ['rɪdl] vt. 充满于,弥漫于
2. fluid ['fluːɪd] n. 流动性,流度
3. voltage ['vəʊltɪdʒ] n. 电压
4. current ['kʌrənt] n. 电流
5. expand [ɪk'spænd] vi. 张开,发展
6. actuator ['æktjueɪtə] n. 执行元件,执行器
7. motor ['məʊtə] n. 电动机
8. deployment [dɪ'plɔɪmənt] n. 展开;配置
9. cocooning [kə'kuːnɪŋ] n. 保护措施
10. sensor ['sensə] n. 传感器
11. signal ['sɪɡnəl] n. 信号
12. meter ['miːtə] vt. 计量(或按规定量)供给
13. detect [dɪ'tekt] vt. 检测
14. amperage ['æmpərɪdʒ] n. 安培数
15. cleaner ['kliːnə] n. 滤清器
16. throttle ['θrɒtl] n. 节流阀
17. thermistor [θɜː'mɪstə] n. 电热调节器
18. thermostat ['θɜːməstæt] n. 节温器
19. resistance [rɪ'zɪstəns] n. 阻抗,电阻
20. initiate [ɪ'nɪʃɪeɪt] v. 启动,开始
21. transaxle [træns'æksl] n. 驱动桥
22. silicon ['sɪlɪkən] n. 硅
23. flex [fleks] v. 弯曲
24. interpret [ɪn'tɜːprɪt] v. 解释,说明
25. knock [nɒk] v. 敲,敲打
26. frequency ['friːkwənsɪ] n. 频率
27. piezoelectric [piːzəʊɪ'lektrɪk] adj. 压电的

Phrases and Expressions

1. feedback loop 反馈回路,反馈环
2. power window 电动车窗
3. Onboard-Diagnostics (OBD) system 随车诊断系统
4. passenger compartment (小客车车身等的)乘坐室
5. ECM 电子控制模块
6. oxygen sensor 氧传感器
7. Air/Fuel (A/F) ratio 空燃比
8. in service 在使用中
9. Mass Air Flow (MAF) sensor 空气质量流量传感器
10. vane air flow meter 叶片式空气流量计

Unit 17　Sensors

11. temperature sensor　温度传感器
12. Engine Coolant Temperature（ECT）sensor　发动机冷却剂的温度传感器
13. Intake Air Temperature（IAT）sensor　进气温度传感器
14. Exhaust Recirculation Gases（ERG）sensor　废气再循环传感器
15. EGR valve position sensor　废气再循环阀片位置传感器
16. Manifold Absolute Pressure（MAP）sensor　歧管绝对压力传感器
17. silicon chip　硅片
18. reference pressure　参考压力
19. Vapor Pressure Sensor（VPS）（燃油）蒸发压力传感器
20. charcoal canister　活性炭罐
21. barometric pressure sensor　大气压力传感器
22. High Altitude Compensator（HAC）高海拔补偿装置
23. knock sensor　爆震传感器
24. piezoelectric element　压电元件

Notes to Text

1. Today's cars are riddled with sensors providing critical data for performance and safety.
现在的汽车上充满了各种传感器，它们为汽车的性能和安全提供了关键性数据。

2. The ECT is usually located in a coolant passage just before the thermostat.
发动机冷却剂的温度传感器通常安置在节温器前的冷却剂通道上。

3. When the silicon chip flexes with the change in pressure, the electrical resistance of the chip changes.
当硅片随着压力的改变而弯曲时，硅片的电阻也发生变化。

4. The ECM needs to know intake manifold pressure to calculate how much fuel to inject, when to ignite the cylinder, and other functions.
电子控制模块需要知道进气歧管的压力，以便于计算燃油喷射量、确定点火时间以及其他的功能。

5. Piezoelectric elements generate a voltage when pressure or a vibration is applied to them.
当压力或振动作用在压电元件上时，它就会产生一个电压。

Exercises

1. Answer the following questions to the text.

（1）What is the function of oxygen sensor?

（2）What are the main components of the MAF sensor?

（3）List three kinds of temperature sensors used and explain the function of each one.

（4）How does the MAP sensor work?

（5）What is the function of the knock sensor?

2. Translate the following phrases and expressions into Chinese.

(1) feedback loop

(2) power window

(3) Onboard Diagnostics (OBD) system

(4) reference pressure

(5) piezoelectric element

(6) temperature sensor

3. Translate the following sentences into Chinese.

(1) The ECM uses an oxygen sensor to ensure the air/fuel ratio is correct for the catalytic converter.

(2) The advantage of using the A/F sensor is that the ECM can more accurately meter the fuel reducing emissions.

(3) The hot wire is maintained at a constant temperature in relation to the thermistor by the electronic control circuit.

(4) The vane air flow meter provides the ECM with an accurate measure of the load placed on the engine.

(5) By measuring engine coolant temperature, the ECM knows the average temperature of the engine.

(6) The knock sensor, located in the engine block, cylinder head, or intake manifold, is tuned to detect that frequency.

Part Ⅲ Listening and Speaking

Information About a New Car A

A—Manager B—Journalist

A: Good afternoon, ladies and gentleman. First of all, on behalf of our company, I'd like to thank you all for coming today. Now I'll tell you that we have developed a remarkable new car.

B: Would you please briefly explain the details about your car?

A: OK. That's our latest development. It was developed by the researchers for five years. It has a nice style.

B: The new car gives you an edge over your competitors, I guess.

A: Certainly.

B: Will you put it on the market recently?

A: Yes, we do.

B: Do you have any plan to sell at abroad?

A: Not at the moment. We are now more concerned with the domestic market.
B: What kind of mileage does it get?
A: Oh, it gets great mileage — 35 miles per gallon on the high way and it has excellent safety features, like dual air bags and ABS brakes.
B: What are ABS brakes?
A: Anti-lock braking system, it keeps you from skidding on the road, and the newer cars have them.
B: OK. That's great. What does it come with standard?
A: On all our new cars, the standards include air conditioning, anti-lock brakes, air bags, and an AM/FM stereo with a CD player. But on the Accord, there is another standard item as well. The Accord comes with cruise control.
B: Cruise control?
A: Yes, I know some of our customers are concerned about cruise control. You don't have to use it, if you don't like it, you can turn it off.
B: That's good enough. What color does the new type have?
A: We have this new model in red, white, black, or silver. These are the standard colors.
B: I see. Thank you.

Information About a New Car B

A—Manager   B—Journalist

A: Now I've told you all about our latest cars, and I'll open the floor to answer any questions you might want to ask.
B: Do you think your old cars are best and are well-received by customers?
A: Yes, of course.
B: Then why do you want to develop a new car now?
A: There are many reasons. A very simple one is that we can't live on old products forever.
B: As you know, no other companies can match us so far as quality is concerned.
A: It sounds good.
B: Do you have any plans to sell in southeast Asia?
A: Not at the moment.
B: What's your next product?
A: I'd like to give you that information, but you may realize it is secretive.

Part IV Reading Material

OBD II and DLC

Introduction of OBD II

OBD stands for Onboard Diagnostics. OBD II is a system that the Society of Automotive Engineers (SAE) developed to standardize automotive electronic diagnosis so technicians could use the same scan tool to test any vehicles model without special adapters. The SAE established guidelines that provide:

• A universal diagnostic test connector, known as the Data Link Connector (DLC), with dedicated pin assignments.

• A standardized location for the DLC, visible under the dashboard on the driver's side.

• A standardized list of Diagnostic Trouble Codes (DTCs) used by all manufacturers.

• The ability of the vehicle system to record a snapshot of operating conditions when a fault occurs.

• Expanded diagnostic capabilities that record a code whenever a condition occurs that effects vehicle emissions.

• The ability to clear stored codes from vehicle memory with the scan tool.

• A glossary of standard terms, acronyms, and definitions used for system components.

In addition, SAE has published hundreds of pages of text defining a standard communications protocol that establishes the hardware, software, and circuit parameters of OBD II systems. Unfortunately, vehicle manufacturers have different interpretations of this standard communications protocol. As a result, the generic OBD II communications scheme used will vary, depending on the vehicle.

SAE publishes recommendations, not laws, but the Environmental Protection Agency (EPA) and the California Air Resources Board (CARB) made many of SAE's recommendations legal requirements that carmakers were required to phase in over a three-year period. Beginning in 1994, vehicles with new engine management computer — about 10% of each manufacturer fleet—were supposed to comply with OBD II standards. For 1995, OBD II systems were to appear on about 40 percent of the new vehicles sold. Some of the 1994~1995 OBD II systems were not fully compliant, so the government granted waivers to give manufacturers time to fine-tune their systems. Beginning in 1996, all new vehicles sold in the USA must be fully OBD II compliant.

The Data Link Connector (DLC)

The DLC is a 16-pin connector. The female half is on the vehicle, and the male end is on the scan tool cable. Pins are arranged in two rows of eight, numbered one to eight and nine to sixteen.

1. Manufacturer's Discretion
2. BUS+LINE, SAE J1850
3. Manufacturer's Discretion
4. Chassis Ground
5. Signal Ground
6. Manufacturer's Discretion
7. K LINE, ISO9141
8. Manufacturer's Discretion
9. Manufacturer's Discretion
10. BUS-LINE, SAE J1850
11. Manufacturer's Discretion
12. Manufacturer's Discretion
13. Manufacturer's Discretion
14. Manufacturer's Discretion
15. L LINE, ISO 9141
16. VEHICLEBATTERY POSITIVE

Seven of the 16-pin positions have mandatory assignments, while vehicle manufacturers can use the remaining nine pins at their discretion. The connector is D-shaped and keyed, so the two halves mate only one way. You should be able to connect to the DLC while sitting in the driver's seat. The DLC cannot be hidden behind panels and must be accessible without the use of tools. Although out of the normal line of sight, the DLC should be clearly visible to a crouching technician.

The DLC is designed for scanning tool access only. You can't jump any of the terminals to display codes on the instrument cluster warning lamp, or Malfunction Indicator Lamp (MIL). The MIL only alerts the driver and the technician that a code has been set.

Index

A

abrasive 96
accelerator 55
accessory 66
actuate 24,156
actuator 55,166
adaptability 55
additional 87
additive 87,96
adversely 77
aerodynamics 106
aid 96
alignment 137
alternator 66
aluminum 87
amperage 166
analogy 147
antifreeze 87
anti-freeze 129
anyway 14
appropriate 45,129
arrange 14
assemble 34
astute 129
atmosphere 34
atomize 45
attenuation 34
automatic 34
axle 137,147

B

backplate 156
band 129

B

bank 14
battery 5
bearing 96
belt 24
body 4
bolt 116
bottom 24
bounce 147
brake 5
braze 87
breaker 66
bump 146
bumper 5
bypass 96
byproduct 77

C

calculate 14
calibration 77
caliper 156
cam 24,55
camshaft 24,34,55
canister 77
carburetor 14,45
catalyst 34,77
cellulose 96
Celsius 87
centimeter 14
centrifugal 87
chain 24
chamber 34
charcoal 77
charge 5
chassis 4

circuit 45,66
circulate 87
clamp 137
clatter 116
cleaner 166
clearance 14,34,156
clog 77
clutch 5,87,116
coast 129
coating 77
cocooning 166
coil 66
collapse 66
column 137
combustible 4
combustion 4,34,55
complexity 129
component 96
condenser 66
conduct 87
configuration 14
conversion 106
cooker 87
coolant 4,55,87
cooler 96
copper 66
core 14
cork 129
corrosion 87,96
crack 146
crankcase 34,96
crankshaft 4,55,116
critical 87
cubic 14
current 66,166
cycle 14
cylinder 4

D

damper 147
deadline 106

decelerate 5
deceleration 77
deflection 147
degree 14
density 34
deployment 166
deposit 96
detect 166
deteriorate 96
diesel 4
diffuser 34
dilute 77
dip 147
dirty 77
disc 5
discharge 45
disengage 66
disengaged 116
displacement 14
disposal 106
dissipate 87,96
distributor 66
divert 77
division 96
doughnut 129
downshift 116
drum 5
ductile 34
dump 106
duplex 96
duration 25
dust 96

E

effort 137
electrochemical 66
electromagnetic 55
emissions 34,55
emit 87
engage 66
engine 4

essentially 107
exhaust 14, 34, 55
expand 166
explode 14
extensive 106
external 96
extract 66

F

Fahrenheit 87
fan 87
fascinating 4
feature 77
fender 5
figure 14
fin 87
flake 96
flange 129
flatten 87
flex 166
flexibility 14
fling 87
floorboard 137
fluid 87, 166
foam 96
forge 137
foul 77
frequency 147, 166
friction 96
fuel 106
fume 77

G

gap 66
gasket 129
gasoline 4
gear 24
gearing 116
generation 55
generator 5
glow 77

governor 129
gradually 106
gravity 106
grip 147
growl 146
guarantee 5, 34
gut 147
gymnastics 129

H

harmonic 34
harsh 147
highlights 55
hollow 137
honeycomb 77
hood 5
horizontal 14
hub 116, 137
hump 129
hybrid 106
hydraulic 5, 34, 129, 156
hydrocarbon 77

I

ignition 4
impeller 34
imperceptible 129
impurity 96
inclination 14
indicator 156
inertia 34, 147
initiate 166
injection 55
injector 45
insulate 66
intake 14
integral 77
interact 5
interfere 34
interference 34
interpret 166

interval 24
introduce 14
iron 66

K

kinetic 156
knock 166
knuckle 137

L

lag 24,55
last 106
latch 129
lawn 14
lead 14
legislation 77
lifetime 106
lifter 24,34
like 147
linear 14,34
linkage 24
liter 14
load 25
loaf 129
lobe 24
lockup 5
longitudinal 87
lower 14
lubricate 4
lubricating 96
lubrication 96,116
luggage 5

M

mandate 107
manifold 34
manipulate 129
manual 116
marvel 129
mass 24,106
maze 129
mechanism 24

memorizer 55
mesh 96
meter 166
mileage 106
minivan 147
modulator 129
monitor 77
monoxide 34
motor 166
mower 14
muffler 34,77
multiply 14

N

navy 96
negative 66
neutral 66,116
nitrogen 14
nozzle 45,55

O

oil 96
oppose 14
optimal 55
originally 14
oscillation 147
out 87
outperform 106
outweigh 106
overall 55
overheat 87
oxidation 34,77
oxide 14
oxidize 96
oxygen 77

P

palladium 77
pan 129
parameters 55
passage 96
passages 129

passageway 87
pavement 146
payload 106
pedal 66
pellet 77
performance 14,77
pervasive 4
piezoelectric 166
pinpoint 129
piping 96
piston 4,156
pitman 137
pivot 147
platinum 77
plunger 55
plumbing 87
plunger 96
pollutant 77
positive 66
precise 137
press 24
pressurize 45
primary 87
profile 24
prolong 34
prone 25
pulse 4
pump 87

Q

quantity 14
quart 129
quarter 14

R

radiator 4,87
reburn 77
recharge 106
reciprocating 14
refinery 106
reinforce 156

reintroduce 77
relay 66
reliability 55
replacement 106
reservoir 156
resist 87
resistance 156,166
resistor 66
resonance 34
revolve 14
riddle 166
ride 147
right 66
rigid 147
rim 137
rod 24
roller 137
rotate 4
rough 77
rub 66
rust 96,106

S

sacrifice 106
scheme 24
seal 129
sealing 34
sedate 106
seep 77
sensor 45,55,166
separate 87
sequence 34
servo 129
sewage 106
shifter 66
shortcoming 106
signal 166
significant 87
significantly 14
silicon 166
simplex 96

simplicity 66
skateboard 147
slam 24
slosh 96
sludge 96
smoothness 14
soak 87
solenoid 25,55,66,129
spark 5
spill 106
spin 24,87
spindle 137,147
spinning 129
splash 96
spoke 137
sponginess 156
sprag 129
spray 45
spring 24
starter 66
status 34
steering 137
strainer 96
strand 66
stroke 14
strut 147
stud 137
submerge 129
subsequent 24
substance 34
suck 87
sump 24
suppose 4
susceptibility 156
suspension 5,146
swivel 147
synchronizer 116

T

tailpipe 77
tamper 77
tank 4
terminal 66,106
thermistor 166
thermostat 87,166
throttle 34,166
thrust 34
timing 24
tire 5
torque 116
tower 66
transaxle 116,129,166
transfer 87
transistor 66
transmission 5,116
transverse 87
trap 77
tune-up 106
turbine 34
turbo 34
turbulence 87
twofold 66

U

underbody 5
uneven 147
unsprung 147
upshift 116

V

valve 14,55
vane 87,96
vaporize 14,45,87
ventilation 34
vibration 45,146
viscosity 87,96
vital 4
volt 66
voltage 4,166

W

waterway 106
wax 87

wear 4,55,87
winding 66
windshield 129
wisely 106
withstand 66,87
worm 137

Y
yarn 96

Z
zero 107